THE SAGAS OF FRIDTHJOF THE BOLD

THE SAGAS OF FRIDTHJOF THE BOLD

translated by Ben Waggoner

Troth Publications
2009

© 2009, The Troth. All rights reserved. No part of this book may be reproduced or transmitted in any form or by any means, electronic or mechanical, including photocopy, recording, or any information storage and retrieval system, without prior permission in writing from the publisher. Exceptions may be allowed for non-commercial "fair use," for the purposes of news reporting, criticism, comment, scholarship, research, or teaching.

A portion of *The Tale of Thorstein Vikingsson* previously appeared in *Idunna*, no. 79.

Published by The Troth
24 Dixwell Avenue, Suite 124
New Haven, Connecticut 06511
http://www.thetroth.org/

ISBN-13: 978-0-557-24020-3

Cover emblem: Ship design from a coin struck in Hedeby, Denmark, ca. 825 CE; found in Birka, Sweden.

Troth logo designed by Kveldulf Gundarsson, drawn by 13 Labs, Chicago, Illinois

Cover design: Ben Waggoner

Typeset in Garamond 18/14/12/10/9

*Dedicated to Steve Abell:
author, patron, colleague, and friend.*

CONTENTS

Introduction   viii

The Saga of Thorstein Vikingsson   1

The Saga of Fridthjof the Bold   55

The Tale of King Vikar   87

Appendix: The Shorter Saga of Fridthjof   107

Notes   130

Bibliography   146

INTRODUCTION

In the 19th century English-speaking world, by far the best-known Old Norse saga was *Friðþjófs saga inn frækni: The Saga of Fridthjof the Bold*. In 1839, *Friðþjófs saga* became the first saga to be completely translated into English, by George Stephens.[1] It was retranslated three times in the 19th century, by William Morris and Eiríkur Mágnusson in 1871[2], Rasmus Anderson and Jón Bjarnasson in 1877[3], and John Sephton in 1893[4]. The saga spawned a host of retellings, adaptations, and derivative works of art that ranged from paintings to symphonies to monumental sculpture.

And then *Friðþjófs saga* virtually fell off the face of the earth.

Through much of the 20th century, both scholarship and popular taste strongly favored the *Íslendingasögur* or "sagas of Icelanders", which deal with the early generations of settlers in Iceland, and the *konungasögur* or "king's sagas", which deal with Scandinavian kings. Both of these types of saga give the appearance of histories, although more or less literary license may have been taken with any given saga. *Friðþjófs saga* is neither of these; it's traditionally grouped with a set of more or less fantastic sagas set in the legendary Scandinavian past, known as *fornaldarsögur*. While some *fornaldarsögur* have always been of interest because they draw on the same material that appears in works such as *Beowulf* or the *Nibelungenlied*, others, including *Friðþjófs saga*, lost much of whatever respect they had. Such "romances" were often labeled "dreary", "decadent", "degenerate", and even "pernicious".[5] Twentieth-century scholars who did mention *Friðþjófs saga* apologized for ever having taken it seriously:

> The saga is mainly a love-story about Friðþjóf and Ingibjörg, and is attractively written, but has not the slightest historical

value. There is much in it about a sanctuary sacred to the god Baldr, but there is little probability that this rests upon any real tradition.[6]

It is a somewhat discouraging confession to make that for a long time this story was regarded as a piece of history; its fanciful construction of political conditions in Norway before the unification of the kingdom was taken as an authoritative picture, and its depiction of a heathen cult in ancient times was used as a source for the history of religion. . . . As a matter of fact, there is no word of historical truth in the whole saga; even the name of the hero is fabricated by the author, no such name ever having existed. . . . the moral idealism pervading this story compares favorably with the best of foreign chivalric romance, and no doubt this is one of the sources of its inspiration.[7]

More recent scholars have begun to re-evaluate the *fornaldarsögur* and other "romantic" sagas. They are now not seen as "degenerate" or "pernicious"; they are not necessarily younger than the "sagas of Icelanders"; and they constitute an important genre in their own right. Even though these sagas have received new attention, scholars of Old Norse literature have still tended to ignore *Friðþjófs saga*; no modern critical edition has been published, and the last English translation, by Margaret Schlauch, was published in 1928.[8] But while it is perhaps not the finest of the legendary sagas, and is not the historical source that some 19th century scholars believed it to be, *Friðþjófs saga* is still worth reading, both for its impact on Romantic-era literature and scholarship, and for its own charm. (And in August 2008, a new musical dramatization of the saga, *Fiend og elskar* [*Enemy and Lover*] by Rolf Losnegaard, was performed outdoors along the Sognefjord. Fridthjof's popular appeal may not be exhausted yet![9])

Friðþjófs saga also provides insights into the development of Icelandic literature. It had long been popular in Iceland, where forty-one manuscripts of the saga have survived, as well as several sets of *rímur* (ballad-like poems) that retell the saga. The saga's oldest manuscripts date to the late fifteenth century, and the saga was copied for as long as the tradition of copying sagas lasted: the latest manuscript copy of

Sagas of Fridthjof

Friðþjófs saga dates from 1899.[10] Actually, *Friðþjófs saga* exists in two main versions, a shorter and probably older version, and a longer, more ornate recension. The shorter version was the basis for the *rímur*, which in turn influenced the longer version. The versions differ in detail; perhaps the most striking difference is that King Hring is a king of Sweden in the older version, but a king of Ringerike in Norway in the younger version.[11] *Friðþjófs saga* influenced at least one other saga, *Víglundar saga*, which is set in Iceland but shares several major plot points with *Friðþjófs saga*: the foster-children who grow up together and fall in love; the woman's brothers' hostility towards the hero; the attempt to kill the hero with a sorcerous storm at sea; and the woman's aged husband who freely gives her to the hero in the end. In turn, the similarities between *Friðþjófs saga* and foreign literature (discussed below) shed light on how foreign stories and motifs were imported, copied, assimilated, and transformed in Icelandic literature.[12]

Existing translations of *Friðþjófs saga* suffer from the Victorian taste for archaic language, which is no longer in vogue and which in some cases tends to obscure the meaning. Thus I felt it worthwhile to present new translations of *Friðþjófs saga*, along with its lesser-known "prequel", *Þorsteins saga Víkingssonar*. The shorter version of *Friðþjófs saga* has never been translated into English, whereas the longer version is the one that stirred the Victorians to flights of fancy. I've chosen to translate and include both, believing that it may be of interest to see how saga texts have shifted and varied through time. I have included one additional text, *Víkars þáttr*, which tells the story of Fridthjof's descendants, and so connects him with the larger body of Norse legend.

What is Friðþjófs saga?

In 1829 and 1830, Carl Christian Rafn published a three-volume collection of thirty-one sagas, under the name *Fornaldar Sögur Norðurlanda*, "Sagas of Olden Times of the Northlands". Although these sagas are quite diverse in style and subject matter, all are set primarily in Scandinavia, and most are set in legendary time, before the unification of Norway under Harald Fair-Hair, Rafn essentially defined the corpus that is still known as the *fornaldarsögur*. Later editions have added some texts that Rafn did not include, but that draw on the same body of legend and

Introduction

folklore as the other *fornaldarsögur*. Finding an objective definition for the *fornaldarsögur*—other than as "the corpus of sagas that Rafn published in his collection"—is not easy, and there has been considerable scholarly debate over whether the *fornaldarsögur* can be called a "genre".[13]

On the one hand, the *fornaldarsögur* are often divided into two different classes. "Legendary sagas," such as *Völsunga saga* and *Hervarar saga*, draw on archaic legendary material and often end tragically. "Adventure tales", such as *Hrólfs saga Gautrekssonar* and *Göngu-Hrólfs saga*, make liberal use of motifs from romances and folk tales, and usually end happily. Sometimes a third class, "Viking sagas", is added for sagas set in the "Viking age" rather than the distant past; *Ragnars saga loðbrókar* is an example of this third type. On the other hand, most *fornaldarsögur* show greater or lesser influence from the *riddarasögur*, "knightly sagas" or "sagas of chivalry". A number of sagas could be put in either class, such as *Hjálmpés saga ok Ölvis*, *Ála-flekks saga*, *Þjalar-Jóns saga*, and others. Other *fornaldarsögur* in the canon, such as the texts now called *Sögubrót* and *Hversu Nóregr byggðist*, are excerpted from *konungasögur*, "kings' sagas", and share material with the more distant and legendary kings' sagas, such as *Ynglinga saga*. Still others overlap with the more "supernatural" or "exotic" *Íslendingasögur*, the "sagas of Icelanders", such as *Barðar saga Snæfellsáss* and *Kjalnesinga saga*, while other *Íslendingasögur* deal primarily with the mundane lives of Icelanders but include episodes that detour into *fornaldarsögur* territory, such as *Gull-Þóris saga* and *Fljótsdæla saga*.

Several scholars have argued that the Old Norse sagas cannot really be partitioned into several genres, but are best thought of as a single genre, albeit with several traditional ways of assembling source materials and stylistic elements.[14] It may be that there is no way to define a partition line between the *fornaldarsögur* and the other traditional genres of saga. On the other hand, Stephen Mitchell has proposed a formal and rigorous definition of *fornaldarsögur*: they are "Old Icelandic prose narratives based on traditional heroic themes, whose numerous fabulous episodes and motifs create an atmosphere of unreality."[15] For Mitchell, *fornaldarsögur* are based on traditional concepts of heroism and heroic action; they are set in remote times; and the action may center on Scandinavia but is free to range widely. Most importantly for our purposes here, *fornaldarsögur* include "major folkloric elements in their structure, in recognition of the fact that these texts are literary hybrids drawing on both popular and learned sources."[16]

Mitchell explicitly excludes *Friðþjófs saga* from the *fornaldarsögur* (along with *Hjálmpés saga ok Ölvis*, *Ála-flekks saga*, and other borderline texts), on the grounds that it is not based on indigenous folklore. He accepts the hypothesis that *Friðþjófs saga* is based on an Arabic story, the *Tale of Urwa and Afrâ*, found in a tenth-century collection known as the *Kitâb al-Agânî*. As in *Friðþjófs saga*, the central couple love each other from childhood; the woman is married off to a wealthy man; the hero visits his beloved and her husband in disguise, under an assumed name; the hero is recognized by a ring that he wears; and the wealthy man is willing to give his wife to the hero. There are several discrepancies, but the similarities seem too many for coincidence.[17] Nor is it extraordinary that an Icelander could have heard a tale from the Arab world; Arabian tales were circulating widely in Europe by the 14th century, and there are several other sagas that contain what look very much like borrowings ultimately derived from Arabic sources.[18]

Marianne Kalinké further suggests that *Friðþjófs saga* may be a response to the tale of Tristan and Isolde. This tale was translated into Old Norse, as *Tristrams saga ok Ísöndar*, by one Brother Robert in 1226; the story was also familiar from Norse translations of other romances, such as the lay *Chievrefeuil*. Like *Tristrams saga*, *Friðþjófs saga* presents a love triangle between a young man, an old king, and a woman in love with the young man but married to the king. However, there is no love potion in *Friðþjófs saga*—Fridthjof and Ingibjorg are free to act as they will. Fridthjof visits Hring's court in disguise to see Ingibjorg, as Tristan visits Mark's court to see Isolde, but Fridthjof does not secretly tryst with Ingibjorg there. The most obvious difference is that *Friðþjófs saga* ends happily, while Tristan and Isolde's story ends tragically. Kalinké points out that *Friðþjófs saga* offers an alternative solution to the problem of Tristan and Isolde, and that it may have been written as an answer to *Tristrams saga*, or even as a criticism of it.[19]

Mitchell makes a good point when he excludes *Friðþjófs saga* from the *fornaldarsögur*. Compared with most other sagas, *Friðþjófs saga* is somewhat unusual. The basic motivation of the plot—a woman is married off to an unwanted husband while her lover is away—is common to many sagas, notably the *skáldsögur* such as *Bjarnar saga Hítdœlakappa* and *Hallfreðar saga vandræðaskálds*. The "illicit love-visits" of a man to seduce a woman,

Introduction

arousing the ire of the woman's family, are a commonplace in these same sagas and others. But Fridthjof is atypically passive for a saga hero; while he takes vengeance against the kings who have married off their sister Ingibjorg (only after they have destroyed his property and tried to kill him), he makes no attempt to win Ingibjorg back. He dutifully goes on his voyage to the Orkneys to collect tribute, even after he has been told that the tribute he collects will be used as dowry for Ingibjorg to marry Hring. Later, far from attempting violence against Hring, he saves Hring's life, and then spares him when he could easily kill him. If *Friðþjófs saga* were a more typical Icelandic saga, Fridthjof would have perhaps tried to make the best of the situation but would eventually have been consumed with desire and jealousy, and either abducted Ingibjorg or done something else violent that would have brought about his own downfall. In the *skaldsaga Gunnlaugs saga ormstungu*, Gunnlaug, like Fridthjof, acquiesces when his beloved is married to another, and lives with the married couple for a while—but in the end, he confronts the husband in battle and is killed. Gunnlaug's acquiescence is what leads to his tragic downfall, whereas in *Friðþjófs saga*, Fridthjof's patience is made into a virtue that is rewarded in the end.[20]

However, there is an alternative way of defining the *fornaldarsögur* that is not based on their literary origins. A salient feature of the corpus of *fornaldarsögur* is that characters from one saga appear, or are referred to, in other sagas. In some cases one saga is written as a sequel (or prequel) to another, usually telling the deeds of the son of the hero of the previous saga. *Friðþjófs saga* follows on from *Þorsteins saga Víkingssonar*, although *Þorsteins saga* was probably written later; other examples would be *Gautreks saga* and *Hrólfs saga Gautrekssonar*, or *Völsunga saga* and *Ragnars saga loðbrókar*, or *Sturlaugs saga starfsama* and *Göngu-Hrólfs saga*, or the four sagas of the "men of Hrafnista". There are other sagas that form a sequence, although the hero of the sequel is not the son of the hero of the earlier saga; an example would be *Hálfdanar saga Brönufostra* and *Sörla saga sterka*. Others illustrate different adventures in the life of one hero, such as Starkad the Old, who appears in *Gautreks saga*, *Norna-Gests þáttr*, and *Sögubrot*. In other cases, one event may be described twice, such as Örvar-Odd's encounter with Angantyr's berserks, which appears in both *Örvar-Odds saga* and *Hervarar saga*.

Friðþjófs saga is clearly linked with its "prequel" *Þorsteins saga Víkingssonar*, but it is also linked with *Víkars þáttr*, the middle section of *Gautreks saga*, which deals with Fridthjof's grandsons and their conflict with King Vikar and Starkad. The beginning of *Þorsteins saga* in turn draws on the legendary material in a genealogical text called *Hversu Nóregr byggðist*, which in turn links to several king's sagas and *fornaldarsögur*. In other words, *Friðþjófs saga* is part of an intertextual network of sagas. Any attempt to reconcile all the *fornaldarsögur* genealogies and dates runs up against impossible contradictions; yet there seems to have been a sense that all these tales were linked into a common "matter of the North", not just by a common setting, but by genealogy and shared legendary history. To the extent that the *fornaldarsögur* can be defined as anything other than "the set of sagas that Rafn published", this is the basis for their definition as a coherent set of sagas.

A modern parallel with the *fornaldarsögur* would be "fan fiction". The most popular science fiction and fantasy books, movies, and TV series—notably *Star Trek*, *Star Wars*, *The Lord of the Rings*, and the *Harry Potter* series of books—have devotees who write stories that take place in these fictional worlds. A quick Internet search can turn up, for example, thousands of stories set in Harry Potter's world, ranging from long back stories of characters who play very minor roles in J. K. Rowling's actual books, to "prequels" and continuations of the basic storyline, to alternative histories—stories set in worlds in which Draco Malfoy's family became the royal family of England, for example—to graphic sexual fantasies about any imaginable combination of characters. The literary quality of these stories varies from very well done to utterly atrocious. Most of the worlds of fan fiction have a primary, authoritative creator of an established canon (generally with the backing of a major media corporation). For the Harry Potter stories, it's J. K. Rowling. For *Star Trek*, it was Gene Roddenberry, and for *Star Wars*, it's George Lucas—although both have left much of the "official" elaboration of their canons to a sizable stable of screenwriters and novelists.

The parallels between the *fornaldarsögur* and "fan fiction" should be clear. Icelandic sagas had no central authority; no one could enforce copyright restrictions on Sigurd the Völsung. Yet there seem to have been certain stories that were widely known and that are referenced in multiple sources—Sigurd the Völsung, Hrolf Kraki, Ragnar Lodbrok, Starkad, Angantyr and Hervör, the Skjöldung and Yngling dynasties—that might be considered analogous to a central "canon" of the *fornaldarsögur*, at least in the earlier period of saga writing. The periphery of the canon, however, was much more open; new characters, themes, storylines, and even "crossovers" could be introduced and expanded upon freely. It's in this "space" that *Friðþjófs saga* and its linked sagas live.

The Legacy of Friðþjóf and Frithiof

The Victorian popularity of *Friðþjófs saga* is inseparable from the popularity of *Frithiofs saga*, a cycle of poems composed by the Swedish author Esaias Tegnér, who as a young boy had read Björner's 1737 Swedish and Latin translations of *Friðþjófs saga* in his collection *Norsk kämpadater*. Several of Tegnér's cantos were published in 1820 in the journal *Idunna*, but the complete cycle did not appear until 1825.

Tegnér's poems took certain liberties with their source. Tegnér wove into his epic details from *Þorsteins saga Víkingssonar*, a "Viking Warrior Code" derived from *Hálfs saga ok Hálfsrekka*, verses from the *Hávamál* and *Völuspá* in the *Poetic Edda*, and details of Norse culture and mythology from a wide range of sources. He greatly expanded several episodes; for example, King Ring's final illness, death, and funeral, which take up two sentences in the saga, are expanded into half of canto XX, with another entire canto (XXI) presenting a funeral dirge. He invented other scenes completely; Ingeborg's lament for Frithiof (canto IX) and Frithiof's soliloquy on his father's burial mound (canto XXIII) have no counterpart at all in the saga.

Most importantly, Tegnér took pains to depict Frithiof in a rather more sentimental and emotional light than the saga does. As Tegnér himself wrote in 1839, to his first English translator George Stephens:

> In the saga we find much that is high minded and heroic, and which, equally demanding the homage of every period, both could and ought to be preserved. But, at the same time, we meet occasional instances of the raw, the savage, the barbarous, which required to be either altogether taken away or to be considerably softened down. To a certain extent therefore, it was necessary to modernize; but just the difficulty here was to find the fitting *lagom*[21]. On the one hand the Poem ought not too glaringly to

offend our milder opinions and more refined habits; but on the other it was important not to sacrifice the national the lively the vigorous and the natural. There could, and ought to, blow through the Song that cold winter-air, that fresh Northwind which characterizes so much both the climate and the temperament of the North. But neither should the Storm howl till—the very quicksilver froze, and all the more tender emotions of the heart were extinguished.[22]

For example, in the original saga, Fridthjof shows no remorse when he burns down the temple of Balder. Tegnér, however, had his Frithiof grieve and repent of his deed, even at the height of his Viking career:

Is the White God enrag'd, let him take his good sword, —
I will fall should it so be decreed;
But he sits in yon sky, gloomy thoughts sending down, —
ne'er my soul from their sadness is freed.[23]

At the end of the cycle, Frithiof rebuilds Balder's temple himself, and at the urging of the wise high priest of Balder, he forgives his enemy King Halfdan, forswears his Viking career, and weds his bride Ingeborg "as before pard'ning Balder's altar both low bend!"[24] The villainous King Helge flees his kingdom and is eventually killed in Finland, by a falling statue of the Finnish god Jumala, while trying to loot his temple. This is all heartwarming, but none of it is in the saga, in which Helgi rebuilds Balder's temple, and Fridthjof later kills Helgi and forces Halfdan to come to terms on pain of death.

Shorn of anything too "barbarous", Tegnér's *Frithiofs saga* was highly acclaimed in the 19th century for its exotic "Northern" nature. Goethe praised Tegnér's *alte, kraftige, gigantischbarbarische Dichtart* ("old, mighty, gigantic-barbaric style of verse").[25] Longfellow found Tegnér's verses sublime; having just returned from study and travel in Sweden, he praised *Frithiofs saga* fulsomely in a review in 1837:

The modern Scald has written his name in immortal runes; not on the bark of trees alone, in the "unspeakable rural solitudes of pastoral song, but on the mountains of his fatherland, and the cliffs that overhang the sea, and on the tombs of ancient heroes, whose histories are epic poems. Indeed we consider the "Legend of Frithiof" as one of the most remarkable productions of the age. . . . He dwells in that land, where the sound of the sea and the midnight storm are the voices of tradition, and the great forests beckon to him, and in mournful accents seem to say, "Why hast thou tarried so long?" Those "ancestral voices" have not spoken in vain. In this spirit the poem has been written, and in this spirit it must be read.[26]

On Tegnér's death in 1846, Longfellow wrote "Tegnér's Drapa," in which he retold the myth of Balder's death, alluded to the myth of Ragnarök and the downfall of the Norse gods, and exhorted poets to do as Tegnér had done, preserving the ancient spirit of "Northernness" without any stain of savagery:

> So perish the old Gods!
> But out of the sea of Time
> Rises a new land of song,
> Fairer than the old.
> Over its meadows green
> Walk the young bards and sing.
>
> Build it again,
> O ye bards
> Fairer than before;
> Ye fathers of the new race,
> Feed upon morning dew,
> Sing the new Song of Love!
>
> The law of force is dead!
> The law of love prevails!
> Thor, the thunderer,
> Shall rule the earth no more,
> No more, with threats,
> Challenge the meek Christ.

Sing no more,
O ye bards of the North,
Of Vikings and of Jarls!
Of the days of Eld
Preserve the freedom only,
Not the deeds of blood![27]

Longfellow had also praised Tegnér's innovation of using a different poetic meter for each canto, writing that "it seems to us a very laudable innovation, thus to describe various scenes in various metre, and not employ the same for a game of chess and a storm at sea."[28] Tegnér's metrical diversity may have influenced his verse retelling of the saga of Olaf Tryggvason in his 1862 book *Tales of a Wayside Inn*, and both the style and the plot of *Frithiofs saga* seem to have influenced *Evangeline*, which is also about two lovers who grow up together but are separated by cruel fate.[29]

Tegnér's *Frithiofs saga* was soon translated into every major European language; there were over twenty English translations, and over twenty into German. As an 1877 review in the *Atlantic Monthly* noted, "in England and in Germany it has become almost a fashion for literary *dilettanti* to win their spurs by some novel maltreatment of Tegnér's great poem."[30] Many of the translations, beginning with George Stephens's, were finely illustrated, and painters such as the Norwegian Peter Nicolai Arbo created canvases based on Fridthjof's story.

Fridthjof inspired art in other media. Tegnér's verses were quickly set to music: the first song settings were written by the composer and clarinetist B. Crusell and published in 1826, with eight more composers following suit in the next ten years. Late Romantic composers wrote a considerable amount of orchestral music inspired by Fridthjof's tales; almost none of these pieces have survived in the repertoire. Yet Heinrich Hofmann's *'Frithiof' Symphony* (1874) was quite popular in the late 19th century, although the prediction that "most of his productions have in them a superficiality of style which makes their duration exceedingly problematical"[31] came true by the end of the century. Max Bruch's cantata *Scenes from the Fridthjof's Saga*, for soloists, chorus, and full orchestra, was also acclaimed in its day[32], as were the overture *Fritjof's Meerfahrt* by the Dutch composer Johan Wagenaar, and another *Frithiof* overture by the

Esaias Tegnér (1782-1846)
From *Frithiof's Saga: A Legend of the North* (1839)

French composer Theodore DuBois. A concert program from 1919 lists no fewer that eight operas about Fridthjof (not all of which had been staged).[33] It doesn't list what might have been the best one: the pioneering Swedish female organist and composer Elfrida Andrée created the opera *Fritiofs saga* in 1898, with a libretto by Selma Lagerlöf (later to become the first woman to win a Nobel Prize). Andrée's opera was never staged, but her orchestral suite from the opera has recently been recorded; it's beautiful, lush Late Romantic music that deserves a wider hearing[34].

Possibly the most famous fan of Fridthjof, or Frithiof, was Kaiser Wilhelm II of Germany. The Kaiser's private yacht regularly visited Sognefjord, the setting of the saga, and the Kaiser himself wrote the poem "Song to Aegir"[35] with direct allusions to Frithiof:

> We sail to dread encounter:
> Lead us o'er surf and strand,
> Through storms and crags and breakers,
> Into our foeman's land. . . .
> As Frithiof on Ellida
> Crossed safely o'er the sea,
> On this our Dragon shield us,
> Thy sons who call on thee.[36]

A musical setting of the poem was performed in England in 1896, and was popular enough to be performed again at King George V's coronation entertainment in 1912, but perhaps the highest praise that it ever received was the comment heard after an 1894 performance in New York: "Well, President Cleveland could not have done it."[37] Kaiser Wilhelm's other commemoration of Fridthjof proved more lasting: in 1913, he presented a large statue of King Beli and a huge statue of Fridthjof to be erected on the shores of Sognefjord, on the presumed sites of Beli's estate (modern Balestrand) and Fridthjof's estate (modern Vangsnes).[38] The statues still stand.

Fridthjof's best-known literary legacy, albeit an indirect one, may well be C. S. Lewis. As a child, he was reading the opening verses of Longfellow's *Tegnér's Drapa*:

> I heard a voice, that cried,
> "Balder the Beautiful
> Is dead, is dead!"[39]

Lewis was immediately struck with the same sort of "Northern" feeling that Tegnér had found in the saga and tried to convey in his poetry, the feeling which Longfellow had praised. As he later wrote:

> I knew nothing about Balder; but instantly I was uplifted into huge regions of northern sky, I desired with almost sickening intensity something never to be described (except that it is cold, spacious, severe, pale, and remote) and then. . . found myself at the very same moment already falling out of that desire and wishing I were back in it.[40]

Lewis called his experience Joy, although he distinguished it sharply from pleasure or fun, and emphasized its similarity with longing and grief. He felt it again, several years later, upon seeing one of Arthur Rackham's illustrations for Wagner's *Ring*: "Pure 'Northernness' engulfed me: a vision of huge, clear spaces hanging above the Atlantic in the endless twilight of Northern summer, remoteness, severity. . ."[41] This touched off a passion for Norse mythology that would later inspire Lewis's Christian theology—as he wrote, "Sometimes I can almost think that I was sent back to the false gods there to acquire some capacity for worship against the day when the true God should recall me to Himself."[42] Lewis maintained his love for Norse myth throughout his life; he studied Norse myth, sagas, and language as a young Oxford don alongside J. R. R. Tolkien, peopled his *Chronicles of Narnia* with Norse giants and dwarfs and monsters, and described himself years later as one "who approached Christianity from a delighted interest in, and reverence for, the best pagan imagination, who loved Balder before Christ and Plato before St Augustine".[43] Arguably, he was touched by the same Romantic vision of the Northlands as Tegnér was. In Tegnér's words, as quoted by William Strong, his first English translator:

> If you prefer the significant and profound, what ministers to seriousness and contemplation; if you delight in the gigantic,

but pale forms which float on the mist, and darkly whisper of the world of the spirits, and of the vanity of all things save true honour—then I must refer you to the hoary—to the saga-stored world of the North, where Vala chanted the key tone of creation, whilst the moon shone upon the cliffs, the brook trilled its monotonous lay, and seated on the summit of a gilded birch, the night-bird sang an elegy upon the brief summer—a dirge over expiring nature.[44]

Why Fridthjof?

Andrew Wawn has explored the question of why Fridthjof's story—whether the original saga or Tegnér's retelling—was so popular in Victorian England. The question is complex; Fridthjof's story was one of several that helped to feed a growing popular interest in Viking-era Scandinavia throughout the 19th century. Popular interest, in turn, increased the appreciation for Fridthjof's story.

One reason for Fridthjof's popularity was its perceived connections with contemporary Britain. A major scene in the saga is set in Orkney, giving the saga a bit more local interest than sagas set wholly in Iceland. The thrilling sea-voyage, with the fearless captain and crew trading quips in the face of disaster, and triumphing against impossible odds in the end, appealed to many readers in the days when Britannia ruled the wave. As Charles A. Vansittart Conybeare wrote—with Iceland and the "sagas of Icelanders" in mind, but certainly applicable to Fridthjof:

> It is truly remarkable, as one author writes, that the "love of bodily exercises, games, hunting, and horse-racing, not to mention the predilection for daring sea-voyages so strongly prevalent amongst Englishmen, was also manifested, according to the Sagas, by the rich and powerful in Iceland." Nor can it be doubted that it is to the seafaring instincts of the same race, that England owes that naval supremacy which has long been her glory, and is still her strength.[45]

More importantly, authors and scholars of the time took an increasing amount of pride in the Scandinavian roots of Britain. Many argued that

Introduction

English liberty, government, and national character owed as much or more to the Norse invaders than to the Anglo-Saxons. For scholars like George Stephens, this attitude went hand-in-hand with a distrust of Germany; there was a certain amount of contemporary politics intertwined with the rising cult of the Old North.[46] As Robert M. Ballantyne wrote at the conclusion of his children's story *Erling the Bold*:

> We have good reason to regard their memory with respect and gratitude, despite their faults and sins, for much of what is good and true in our laws and social customs, much of what is manly and vigorous in the British Constitution, and much of our intense love of freedom and fair-play, is due to the pith, pluck, enterprise, and sense of justice that dwelt in the breasts of the rugged old Sea-kings of Norway![47]

Fridthjof could be seen in this light as not only pithy, plucky, and enterprising, but the very model of a constitutional monarchist. He is properly deferential towards rulers, but never servile; while unafraid to reject the authority of unjust and tyrannical kings, he does not strike the first blow, but waits until he has been truly and grievously wronged. When offered King Hring's kingship, the well-born but not royal Fridthjof refuses any title higher than that of jarl; he does not accept royal rank until he has finally defeated his adversaries and forced them to accept the title. Tegnér brings out this point more forcefully than the original saga does; his dying King Beli gives this advices to his sons:

> His own good land who'd fain oppress—
> Is but a simple man;
> For Kings can do, as all confess,
> But what their People can.[48]

Fridthjof's popularity also owed a great deal to its religious outlook. The saga is set in pagan times, but Balder, the chief god worshipped in the great temple, is the most "Christ-like" of the Norse gods—at least as depicted by the 13th-century Icelandic author Snorri Sturluson, whose *Prose Edda* collects and systematizes Norse mythology. In Snorri's version of the myths, Balder is a son of the high god Odin, *svá fagr álitum ok bjartr, svá at lýsir af honum* —"so fair of appearance and bright, that light shines from him."[49] Balder is called the wisest and best of all the gods, and yet strangely ineffectual; *sú náttúra fylgir honum, at engi má haldast dómr hans*—"this nature goes with him, that his judgments cannot stand." Balder dies young and tragically, lives on in Hel (the Norse realm of the dead), and, it is said, will return after the Last Battle at the end of the world to inaugurate a glorious and peaceful new age. Snorri's portrayal of Balder was influenced by Christianity, as was the Old English poem *Dream of the Rood*, which describes the Crucifixion in terms drawn from myths of Balder and Odin.[50] Not all old sources make Balder to be Christlike—Saxo Grammaticus's *History of the Danes* presents a story of "Balderus" that, while recognizably related to Snorri's version, does not show Balder in a particularly meek or holy light.[51] But Tegnér and many other commentators on Norse mythology explicitly made Balder a forerunner of Christ. As the high priest of Balder tells Fridthjof, near the end of Tegnér's poem:

> In lands far south, 'tis said,
> Is some new Balder worshiped, —
> He, the pure virgin's son from heav'n who sped,
> Sent by the Allfather's self . . .
> . . . His pious days
> In sweet instruction pass'd, or pray'r or praise;
> And when he died, his dying voice forgave, —
> And now, 'neath far-off palms, still stands his shining grave.
> This doctrine, say they, spread o'er ev'ry land,
> Melting hard hearts and joining hand in hand,
> And on this earth, now reconcil'd again,
> Upraising gentle peace's wide domain.
> Not yet! alas!
> Hath human lip to mine ag'd ear explain'd aright
> This creed; but still, when better moments o'er me pass,
> My dim gaze darkly sees afar its streaming light.[52]

None of this is found in the original saga, in which Balder is not a living presence and plays no real role in the saga (his name could be replaced with that of almost any other god, and nothing would change).

Nor does this view of Balder have much support from history; there is some evidence, primarily from place-names, for a cult of Balder in pre-Christian Scandinavia, but it does not seem to have been widespread.[53] But with Tegnér's interpretation, a reader could enjoy the exotic flavor of pagan rituals and wicked magic, while not having to sympathize with anything that wasn't consistent with Christianity after all. Fridthjof, like several other saga heroes, is not especially devout, but Tegnér and his other admirers were easily able to make him into a proto-Christian, while the devout heathen King Beli and the magic-wielding witches ends up killed.

Finally, as any Gilbert and Sullivan aficionado knows, love crossing social class boundaries was a popular Victorian theme. It's not that hard to imagine the Victorian-era Fridthjof singing "A [Viking] tar is a soaring soul, / As free as a mountain bird; / His energetic fist should be ready to resist / A dictatorial word," from *H.M.S. Pinafore*. Or perhaps, from *Pirates of Penzance*, "Did ever [Viking] loathed / Forsake his hidden mission / To find himself betrothed / To lady of position?"

Þorsteins saga Víkingssonar

Þorsteins saga Víkingssonar—The Saga of Thorstein Viking's Son—recounts the heroic deeds of Fridthjof's grandfather and father, although it was certainly written after *Friðþjófs saga*. In contrast to *Friðþjófs saga*, *Þorsteins saga* is a fairly uncontroversial example of a *fornaldarsaga*, filled to the brim with the expected stock motifs, not always assembled with skill and taste. *Þorsteins saga* gives the impression that the compiler threw in every interesting tale and motif that he could find. There are magic swords, magic ships, giants, berserks, quests, fierce Vikings, and beautiful maidens. Several motifs are used more than once. There are two helpful dwarves; two crossings of uncrossable mountains; two captives left alive through the night who escape through magic and kill their guards; two times when the heroes break into their enemies' huts; and four cases in which two men swear brotherhood when they find that neither can beat the other in combat.

Most of these repeated motifs are "standard issue" for *fornaldarsögur*. Some motifs are drawn from the *riddarasögur*, such as the scenes in the exotic location of India. The hero or villain who crosses an uncrossable mountain to meet a king turns up in "king's sagas"[54] and in *riddarasögur*[55]. In one episode, Thorstein grapples a monster in an underwater battle, kills it with a special weapon, and horrifies his fellows when the monster's gore bubbles up to the surface. This is immediately recognizable as analogous to Beowulf's slaying of Grendel's mother. In fact, there are several saga episodes in which a hero fights a giant in a watery environment; in some of them (*Grettis saga*, *Samsons saga fagra*), the giant's blood and guts float to the surface and dismay the hero's supporters.[56] Thorstein's befriending and marrying a hideous giantess who has saved him from certain death, and who is actually a princess turned hideous by an enchantment, is paralleled by episodes in *Illuga saga Gríðarfostra* and *Gríms saga loðinkinna*, and in general by the folktale motif of the Loathly Lady,[57] possibly with influence from Celtic myths of the Goddess of Sovereignty.[58]

This saga also has structural links with the "sagas of Icelanders". Whereas typical *fornaldarsögur* and *riddarasögur* focus on the life and deeds of a single hero, *Þorsteins saga*, like many *Íslendingasögur*, explores the workings of both friendship and revenge between families down through several generations.[59] The theme of a villain acquiring an innocent man's women and goods by challenging him to a duel is well-known in the sagas of Icelanders; in many cases he is a berserk, like Ljot in *Egils saga*[60] or Asgaut in *Víga-Glúms saga*[61] or Surt and Randvid in *Flóamanna saga*[62]. The theme of the hero who leaves his betrothed behind while he goes adventuring, and then loses her while he is away, is found in the *skáldsögur* or "sagas of poets" such as *Gunnlaugs saga ormstungu* and *Bjarnar saga Hítdælakappa*.

None of these motifs is allowed to dominate the plot of *Þorsteins saga*. Viking's winning, loss, and recovery of his bride is an important part of the plot of the first chapters—but *Þorsteins saga* cannot be called a "bridal-quest romance", as the search for a bride is not a major motivator of the entire plot. Towards the end, Thorstein is rescued and healed by a giantess, and ends up marrying her—but the saga is not a "giant fosterage" saga, like *Hálfdans saga Brönufostra* or *Illuga saga Gríðarfostra*. Instead, *Þorsteins saga* exemplifies what O'Donoghue called the "runaway invention", "capacious plot", and "kaleidoscopic quality" of the *fornaldarsögur*.[63] Like many *fornaldarsögur*, *Þorsteins saga* has such diverse contents that it switches genres[64], passing from bridal-quest to heroic romance to family saga and back.

Introduction

The seemingly jumbled nature of this saga has not endeared it to critics. As early as 1680, the Danish antiquarian Thomas Bartholin condemned this saga as "putrid" and a "stupid fable"[65]. Margaret Schlauch called it "fantastic and incoherent"[66], and Andrew Wawn dismissively referred to it as "later and lamer" than *Friðþjófs saga*.[67] To the best of my knowledge, no one has yet tried to turn *Þorsteins saga* into an epic poem, to say nothing of an opera. Yet it was at least as popular in Iceland as *Friðþjófs saga*, if not more so: no fewer than sixty-five manuscripts of *Þorsteins saga* survive, written between the early 15th century and 1889, along with no fewer than six surviving *rímur*.[68] The writer of the saga text translated here called it *in gamansamligasta*—"the most enjoyable." Icelanders gathered on cold winter nights must have relished the saga's exotic coloring, complex plot, and undeniable flair and gusto, especially when told by a good saga-teller who could breathe life into the tale.[69]

Víkars þáttr

The longer version of the legendary *Gautreks saga* consists of three sections, distinct both in content and in style. Traditionally these are called *Gauta þáttr*, *Víkars þáttr* and *Gjafa-Refs þáttr*. *Gauta þáttr* and *Gjafa-Refs þáttr* are close to folk tales; they end happily and include various comic turns. *Víkars þáttr*, in contrast, is a *fornaldarsaga*-like tale with a tragic ending. Whereas the other two sections contain relatively little poetry, *Víkars þáttr* closely follows a long poem, *Víkarsbálkr* ("Vikar's Piece" or "Vikar's List"), ostensibly written by its protagonist Starkad. In places the prose is little more than a retelling of the poetic stanzas, and the tale resembles some of the poems with intercalated prose of the *Poetic Edda*. Finally, *Víkars þáttr* is not found in the oldest version of this saga, but seems to have been inserted later, and only one character, Jarl Neri, links *Víkars þáttr* with the rest of the saga.[70] For all of these reasons, it seemed fitting to present it here as a separate tale, since it connects Fridthjof's family with the legends of the great and tragic warrior Starkad the Old.

As stated above, both sagas exist in multiple manuscripts, and as yet no critical edition of either *Friðþjófs saga* or *Þorsteins saga* has been published. The Norse text of *Þorsteins saga* that I have used is the text published in Guðni Jónsson and Bjarni Vilhjálmsson's *Fornaldarsögur Norðurlanda*[71], which is based on Rafn's 1830 edition[72], which in turn is derived from the 15th century manuscript *AM 152 fol.* Jónsson and Vilhjálmsson's *Fornaldarsögur Norðurlanda* also includes the shorter version of *Friðþjófs saga*[73]; this is based on the 15th century manuscript *AM 510 4to*. The longer version of *Friðþjófs saga* is translated from Ludvig Larsson's 1901 edition[74], which was based on the 17th century paper manuscript *Papp. 17 4to*, Kunglinga biblioteket, Stockholm. *Víkars þáttr* follows the younger version of *Gautreks saga* as published in *Fornaldarsögur Norðurlanda*[75]; this was based on Ranisch's edition[76], which in turn used several manuscripts that derive from a common source, the oldest of which is *AM 152 fol.*

The two versions of *Friðþjófs saga* share many poetic stanzas (usually with minor variation between the two versions) and some, although relatively few, prose phrases. I've taken care to translate the parallel passages identically, with variants in the Norse texts shown by variants in the translations. In a few instances, I couldn't find a way to do this without excessive awkwardness.

I thank Steve Abell, Dan Campbell, and Arielle Finberg for their encouragement, inspiration, and editorial commentary. All errors in this book are entirely my own. I thank Zoe Borovsky, Sean Crist, P. S. Langeslag, Stefan Langeslag, Andy Lemons, Carsten Lyngdrup Madsen, and Jon Julius Sandal, who have created freely available electronic resources that were absolutely crucial for me to do my work. Last but not least, I thank Patricia Lafayllve for her encouragement, and Amanda Waggoner for her love and support.

> *Þarf ok engi meira trúnað á at leggja,*
> *en hafa þó gleði af, á meðan hann heyrir.*

THE SAGA OF THORSTEIN VIKINGSSON

CHAPTER I

So begins this saga: There was a king who was called Logi. He ruled over the land which lies north of Norway. Logi was bigger and stronger than anyone else in the land. His name was lengthened, and he was called Halogi.[1] The land took its name from him, and was called Halogaland.

Logi was the most handsome of all men. In his strength and size he took after his kinfolk, because he was of giant-kin[2]. He married Glod, the daughter of Grim from Grimsgard, from Jotunheim in the north, which then was called Elivagar[3] in the north.

Grim was the greatest berserk. He married Alvor, the sister of Alf the Old. Alf ruled over that realm which lies between two rivers; they took their name from him, and both were called "Alf". One was called the Gautalf, which was south of the land of King Gaut and divides it from Gautland. And one was called the Raumalf, which was in the north and was named for King Raum, whose kingdom was called Raumariki.[4] The realm which King Alf ruled was called Alfheim, and the people who are descended from him are all alf-kin. They were more handsome than other folk, except for the giant-folk.[5] King Alf married Bryngerd, the daughter of King Raum of Raumariki. She was a large woman, but not beautiful, because King Raum was ugly. Men who are ugly and large are called great "raums."[6]

King Halogi had two daughters with Glod, his queen. One was named Eisa, and the other was Eimyrja. They were more beautiful than any other maidens in the land. They took after their father and mother. And because fire and light brighten a place that formerly was dark, these things took names from the aforementioned folk.[7]

There were two jarls with Halogi. One was named Vifil, and the other was Veseti. They were both big and strong men. They guarded the king's lands. One day, the jarls went before the king, and Vifil asked to marry Eimyrja, and Veseti asked for Eisa. The king refused them both. They became very angry at that, and so a little while later they carried the king's daughters off and fled from the land. They shunned meeting with him, because he made them outlaws from his kingdom, and he had a spell cast so that they should never be settlers there, and he established that their kinsmen should be just as outlawed from their own estates.

Veseti settled in that island or isle which is called Bornholm. He was the father of Bui and Sigurd Cape.[8] Vifil sailed farther east and settled on the island called Vifilsey. He had a son with Eimyrja, his wife, who was named Viking. Early in his life, he grew tall, and was stronger than other men.

CHAPTER II

There was a king named Hring. He was a shire-king in the Swedish realm. He had a queen and one daughter, a child named Hunvor. She was the loveliest and most accomplished of all women. She had a great bower and a retinue of maids for herself. The maid who was closest to her was named Ingibjorg, the daughter of Jarl Herfinn of Ullarakr[9]. Most men reckoned that Ingibjorg wasn't inferior to the king's daughter in any respect, except in breeding and wisdom, in which Hunvor surpassed everyone in the land. Many kings and kings' sons asked for her in marriage, and she showed them all the door. Everyone thought that her haughtiness and arrogance were beyond measure, and many men reckoned that something would happen that would set her back. Some time now went by.

A mountain lay behind the king's residence. It was so high that no paths for people went over it. One day a man came over the mountain—if you could call him a man.[10] He was bigger and uglier than anyone had ever seen, more like a giant than a human being. In his hand he had a double-pointed pike. At the time when the king was sitting at the table, this ogre went to the hall doors and asked to come in, but the guards at the door refused. He stabbed them with his pike, so that each point skewered one guard through the chest and out through the back. Then he heaved both guards up over his head and flung their corpses a long way into the courtyard, and then went inside. He went before the king's high seat and said, "Since I have esteemed you so highly, King Hring, that I have come to visit your home, it seems to me that you are obliged to grant my request."

The king asked what his request was, and what his name was. He answered, "I am called Harek Ironskull.[11] I am the son of Kol Crookback[12], the king of India, and my message is that I want you to give me power over your daughter, land, and retainers. Most people will say that the kingdom will be on a better footing if I govern it rather than you, who are too elderly and lacking in manhood. But because it seems somewhat of an offense for you to give up the kingdom, then, in exchange, I'll grant you the favor of marrying your daughter Hunvor. If you don't like that, I will kill you, take your kingdom, and have Hunvor for a concubine."

Now the king felt that he had a huge problem on his hands, because all the people were distressed at their conversation. The king said, "I think the best thing is for us to find out how she will answer." Harek said that he approved.

Hunvor was then sent for, and the request was put to her. She said, "I am well pleased with this man, but I think that it may be that he will be bad-tempered to me, although he is a fitting match for me in every way. Yet I want to ask whether there is any possibility of redemption."

"I will do that," said Harek. "If the king will fight a duel with me no later than three nights from now, or get a man to fight in his place, then whoever kills the other in the duel shall possess everything."

Hunvor said, "It's certain that one who could beat you in single combat can't be found. Nonetheless I will agree to it."

Harek turned and left, but Hunvor went to her bower and wept bitterly. The king asked his men whether anyone wanted to try for a marriage with his daughter by fighting Harek. But although the marriage seemed good, no one wanted to try, because everyone thought it would be certain death. Many reckoned that it served her right, as many men as she had sent away, and now her pride would be humbled if she had to marry Harek.

Eymund was the name of her serving-man. He was faithful to her and trusty in all situations. She summoned him one day and said, "I cannot stay quiet any longer. I will send you. You must take a ship and row to the island that lies out beyond Ullarakr, which is called Vifilsey.

A house stands there on the island. You must go there, and arrive next evening, at about the time of sunset. You must go into the house by the west door. When you come in, you will see a spry old man and an elderly woman. No other people will be there. They have a son named Viking. He is now fifteen years old, and the most accomplished of men. He won't be on the lookout for you. Either we will have our case set right, or else I think I will suffer a disgrace. Don't let them see you, but if it turns out that you should see a third person, throw this letter in his lap and come home right away."

Eymund moved quickly and went to the ship with twelve men, and came to Vifilsey. He alone went onto land and went to the house and found the hearth-room, and stood behind the door. The farmer and the lady of the house were sitting by the fire. The farmer looked like a warrior to him. The fire had burned to ashes, and he couldn't see clearly.

The lady began to speak: "I suppose, my dear Vifil, that it will be good for us if Viking, our son, should come forward, because no one will step up, and soon it will be time for the duel with Harek."

"That doesn't seem wise to me, Eimyrja", he said, "for our son is young and brash, impetuous and not prudent. It will quickly be the death of him if he lets himself be tricked into fighting Harek. But you must decide this."

A short while later, the door sprang open behind the farmer's back. A man, remarkably great in size, came out and sat down next to his mother. Eymund threw the letter onto Viking's knee and rushed out at once, and got to the ship and came to Hunvor and told her how his errand had gone. She said that fate would decide.

Viking took the letter, and on it there was a greeting from the king's daughter. Along with that was the proposal that she would marry him if he would fight Harek Ironskull. Viking blushed at that, and when Vifil saw that, he asked what it was. Viking showed him the letter.

"I know this", said Vifil, "and it would have been better if I had decided this a little while ago, Eimyrja—what do you think about it?"

Viking said, "Wouldn't it be good to free the king's daughter?"

Vifil said, "It's quick death for you, if you fight Harek."

"I'll risk it," said Viking.

"Then there is nothing to be done", said Vifil. "But I can tell you about Harek's kinfolk and about him himself."

CHAPTER III

"Tirus the Great was a king over India. He was an excellent leader in every respect. He had a splendid queen and one girl-child, who was named Trona. She was the loveliest of all women, unlike most women because of her wisdom. She surpassed all other kings' daughters.

"A man should also be named in this story; he was named Kol. There are many notable things to say about him. First of all, he was as big as a giant, as ugly as the devil, and such a sorcerer that he could travel into the earth as well as on it. He could hitch a star to a stud-horse. He was such a great shape-shifter that he could take on the appearance of any living creature. He could travel equally well with the winds or through the sea. His spine curved so high above his shoulders that if he stood upright, his hump was higher than his head. He traveled to India with a great host and killed Tirus, but married Trona, and took the land and retainers under his rule and made himself king over them. He had many children with Trona, and they took after their father's side of the family, more than their mother's.

"Kol was called Crookback. He had three valuable possessions. One was a sword, such a good treasure that no better one was carried at that time. The sword was named Angrvadil. Another treasure was a gold ring named Glaesir. The third was a horn. Such was the nature of the drink in the lower half of the horn, that whoever drank from it got the sickness that's called leprosy, and such a great forgetfulness that he didn't remember anything which had happened before. But if the drink came from the upper end of the horn, then he got better right away.

"The oldest of their children was Bjorn Bluetooth. A tooth of his was blue in color and stuck one and a half ells out of his mouth. He often killed men with it in battle, or when he was angry. Kol's daughter was named Dis.[13] The third of their children was named Harek. When he was seven, he was bald all over his head. His skull was as hard as steel; for that, he was called Ironskull. The fourth of the children was named Ingjald. His upper lip stuck out an ell in front of his nose. For that, he was called Ingjald Snout. This was how the brothers amused themselves at home: Bjorn Bluetooth would stab his tooth into the skull of Harek his brother, as hard as he could, and he never harmed him. No weapon ever damaged the lip of Ingjald Snout. Kol Crookback had sorcery[14] worked so that no weapon could slay any of his offspring, except for the sword Angrvadil. No other iron can bite them.

"When Kol was quite old, he died a bad death. Trona was pregnant then, and she gave birth to a son who was named Kol, after his father. He was as much like to his father as he was related to him. Ever since Kol was one year old, he was very ill-disposed to young people. He was called Kol the Crafty. Dis was given in marriage to Jokul Ironback. He was a black berserk.[15] The siblings divided their father's inheritance. Dis was allotted the horn, but Bjorn Bluetooth got the sword, Harek had the ring, Ingjald took the kingdom, and Kol got the movable property. Three years after the death of King Kol, Trona was given in marriage to Jarl Herfinn, the son of king Hrodmar of Marseraland[16], and he had a son with her in that first year, who was named Framarr. He was a promising lad, unlike his brothers.

"Now it seems to me", said Vifil, "that you shouldn't risk your life at the hands of this man from Hel, whom iron doesn't wound."

"It can't be that way", said Viking, "I shall chance it, however it goes."

When Vifil saw that he was serious about fighting Harek, then he said to him: "Then I will tell you more about the sons of Kol. Veseti and I had the task of defending the lands of King Halogi. The two of us went out raiding in the summer. On one occasion, we met Bjorn Bluetooth in Graeningjasund[17], and we fought him this way: Veseti struck Bjorn's hand with his club, so that the sword fell out of his hand. Then I grabbed the sword and ran him through with it, and so he lost his life. I have carried the sword ever since, and now I will give it to you, son." Then he got the sword and gave it to Viking. He was very pleased with it.

At once, Viking prepared himself and traveled alone in his boat. That same day he came to the king's hall where the duel was to be. Everything there was silent and downcast. Viking went before the king and greeted him. The king asked his name. Viking told the truth. Hunvor sat on one side of the king. Viking asked whether she had summoned him there. She said that it was true.

Viking asked what stakes he should have to duel with Harek. The king said, "You shall have my daughter with a handsome dowry."

Viking agreed to this. He betrothed himself to Hunvor. Most thought that Viking was doomed to die if he fought with Harek.

CHAPTER IV

Then Viking went to the duel. The king followed with his household. Harek came up and asked who would fight him. Viking came forward and said "Here he is."

Harek said, "It seems a paltry thing to kill you on the field, because I know that you're dead if I strike you with my fist."

"I suppose that you're counting the reasons not to fight me", said Viking, "since you're afraid, now that you've seen me."

Harek said, "That's not so. I have to save your life, since you yourself want to walk right into Hel's open mouth. You strike first, as the dueling laws state, since I have called for the duel. Meanwhile, I will stand calmly, because I am not afraid that it will hurt me."

Viking now drew Angrvadil, and it was as if lightning flashed from it. And when Harek saw that, he said, "I should never have fought you, had I known that you had Angrvadil. In all likelihood it will turn out as my father said, that we brothers and sisters must be short-lived, except for the one who bore his name. It was the greatest misfortune when Angrvadil went out of our family."

And with that, Viking struck Harek's skull from above and cleaved him completely in two, so that the sword plunged down into the earth up to the hilt. The king's men shouted a great cheer of victory. The king went home to his hall in triumph. Then it was said that his daughter should prepare for the wedding, but Viking said that he didn't want that—"she must wait, betrothed, for three years, and I will go raiding."[18]

And so it was done. Viking sailed away from the land with two ships, and he was successful because he had victory in every battle. When he had been raiding for two years, he laid his ship up at a certain island in the autumn. The weather was good and very warm.

CHAPTER V

That same day, Viking went onto land alone to amuse himself. He turned towards the forests. He felt very warm. And when he came to a fair glade, he sat down and saw that a woman was walking by. She was quite beautiful. She came to him and greeted him in a most seemly fashion, and he welcomed her. They talked for a long time, and their conversation went in a most friendly way. He asked her name, and she said she was called Solbjort.[19] She asked whether he wasn't thirsty, since he had walked a long way. Viking answered that he was not. She took a horn from under her cloak and invited him to drink, and he took it and drank. After that he became sleepy, and he reclined on Solbjort's lap and fell asleep.

But when he woke up, she had gone away. He felt quite confused by the drink. He felt a great shivering in his chest. The weather was gusty and cold, and he could remember almost nothing that had happened before, and Hunvor least of all. He went to the ship and sailed away. Then he came down with a terrible sickness and was bedridden by his illness, which is called leprosy. They sailed far and wide, away from the land, because they didn't want to settle down anywhere. When he had lain sick for twelve months, it began to oppress him greatly, and many sores broke out on his body.

One day, when they anchored next to land, they saw seven ships sailing off the harbor. And when they met, each asked the other their names. Viking gave his name, and the other who was in front of him called himself Halfdan, son of Ulf. Halfdan was a big and strong man, and as soon as he found out what had happened to Viking, he went on board Viking's ship. Viking had little strength.

Halfdan asked how his sickness had occurred, and Viking told him everything that had happened. Halfdan answered: "The shapeshifter Dis, Kol's daughter, has come with her tricks. I think it will take a long time to get justice from her, because she must think that she has avenged Harek Ironskull, her brother. Now I will offer you sworn brotherhood, and find out whether we two may not get revenge on Dis."

Viking answered: "I gave myself no hope of destroying Dis or her husband Jokul Ironback, because of my sickness. But you seem to me like the sort of man that it would be well to swear brotherhood with, because of your manliness, even if I were able to swagger around." So it was decided, and they swore brotherhood with each other.

Halfdan had a great dragon-ship called Ironprow. It was all plated with iron above the waterline, riding high in the water. It was the best of possessions. They had not been there for long before they went away to Swabia[20]. Viking's strength had dwindled, so that he became deathly ill.

But when they came to land, Halfdan went alone from the ship, until he came to a clearing. There stood a single great stone. He went to it and knocked on it with his stick. The dwarf who had his home there, who was named Lit, came out. They were great friends. He greeted him happily and asked what his errand might be.

Halfdan said, "I think it's very urgent, foster-father, that you do my errand now."

"What is that, foster-son?" said Lit.

"I want for you to get the good horn of Dis, Kol's daughter."

"You try it," said Lit, "because that will be the death of me if I try to get that. I can't get it at all, because you know that there's no troll like Dis in all the world."

"It seems urgent now," said Halfdan.

"How can I run this risk," said Lit, "even though I give my life for it?"

"You'll do fine," said Halfdan.

They parted for the time being. Halfdan went to the ship and stayed there for a while.

CHAPTER VI

Now there is this to say about King Hring: he and Hunvor, his daughter, stayed in their kingdom after the death of Harek Ironskull. Everyone felt that it had been a great deed of bravery. News of it was heard in India, and Harek's death seemed to Ingjald Snout to be a great loss. He began to carve the war-arrow[21] and sent it through all the land, and he summoned a great multitude. His army was a huge mob, and he sailed with all of this host to Sweden. There was no advance warning of his coming. He challenged the king to battle. The king set out quickly and had few men, but nonetheless he went to battle, and the tide soon turned against him. King Hring and all his retinue fell there, and Ingjald took Hunvor away to India. Jokul Ironback searched for the sworn brothers and wanted to avenge Harek, his brother-in-law.

Now the story goes on that Viking and Halfdan were in Swabia. When seven nights had passed, Lit came to meet with Halfdan, and he had the horn. Halfdan was glad, and he went to Viking. Most people thought that Viking had little longer to live. Halfdan dripped drink from the upper part of the horn onto his lips. Then Viking recovered his senses, and he began to get stronger; it was as if he was awakening from sleep. And the uncleanliness fell away from him like scales off a fish, and so he recovered day by day, until he was well.

Then they made ready to leave Swabia, and sailed northward for the Balagard coast.[22] There they saw eighteen ships, all large, covered with black tents.

Halfdan said, "I believe that Jokul Ironback and his shape-shifter wife lie here before us. I don't know how Lit got away from them. He was very puny. But now I will advise that we head into battle. We must carry our stores of wealth away from the ships, but put in pebbles instead."

So it was done. Then they rowed at them fiercely, and asked them to tell what kin they came from. Jokul told them his name and asked who they were. Halfdan and Viking told their names. There's no need to ask what happened then—fighting broke out. It was the most furious battle. There was slaughter on the sworn brothers' side, because Jokul was dealing huge blows.

Then Viking rushed to board Jokul's ship, and Halfdan was there behind him. There was a great slaughter on the dragon-ship. Jokul and Halfdan met each other and fought, trading blows. Jokul was stronger, yet Halfdan struck a blow across Jokul's back with his sword. It didn't cut, although Jokul was not in armor. Just then, Viking came and struck at Jokul. That blow landed on his shoulder-joint and cut from his side one arm and both legs, one of them above the knee.

Jokul fell, but he wasn't dead. He said, "I knew that Dis's luck had turned bad, so that much evil would follow. First of all, the wicked Lit betrayed her and came with his own tricks to steal the horn from her, and he injured her. Now she's bedridden from their encounter—but I suppose that it won't have done him any good. It would not have gone that way if she had been on foot. But it makes me laugh that you haven't taken Hunvor the king's daughter from Ingjald Snout, my brother-in-law."

A moment later, he died. Viking and Halfdan raised the victory-shout, and granted a truce to the men who could be healed. They took much booty, and they found Dis on land, barely alive from her encounter with Lit. They seized her and drew a bag over her head and stoned her until they sent her to Hel.[23] Then they set sail to Swabia and let their own men heal. And because they were outfitted with twenty-four ships, all well equipped with crews and weapons, they announced that they intended to sail for India.

CHAPTER VII

Ingjald Snout made great preparations. He had the city walls strengthened, and summoned a great crowd of people, a huge rabble. As soon as the sworn brothers came to land, they burned and raided. Everyone was terrified of them. They did the greatest ravaging before Ingjald found out. Then he moved against them, and when they met, they began the battle. It seemed to Halfdan and Viking that they had never faced such a trial. The sworn brothers proved their worth manfully, and as the battle went on, Ingjald's side began to suffer more casualties. This battle lasted for four days. At last, Ingjald alone was left standing. They couldn't make a wound on him, and it almost seemed to them that he could travel in the air as well as on land.

In the end, they pressed their shields down on him and captured him. Then he was imprisoned in fetters, with a bowstring tied around his hands. By then it was so dark at night that they decided not to kill him; Viking didn't want to commit murder by killing him at night[24]. They charged into the town and took Hunvor and Ingibjorg and brought them to the ships. They anchored there for the night. In the morning the watchmen were dead, and Ingjald had gone—but the iron fetters lay behind, unbroken, and the bowstring wasn't untied. No marks of weapons were visible on the watchmen. It appeared that Ingjald had shown his sorcery.

Now they hoisted sails and sailed out of the harbor and home to Sweden. Viking had a wedding feast prepared and went to marry Hunvor. Then Halfdan began his suit and asked for Ingibjorg, the jarl's daughter. Word was sent to Jarl Herfinn at Ullarakr, and when the jarl came, he welcomed the engagement. Halfdan married Ingibjorg as they had planned, and at once a feast was arranged and their marriage was contracted.

They stayed there through the winter. In the summer they sailed away to raid. They had ten ships, and they raided all around the eastern realms. They gained a lot of wealth for themselves, and sailed home in the autumn. For three summers they went raiding and sailed home for the winter. No men were more famous than they.

One summer, they sailed to Denmark. They raided there and sailed their ships into the Limfjord.[25] They saw nine ships anchored there, and a dragon-ship which was the tenth. They steered toward the ships and asked who was in command. The commander gave his name as Njorfi—"and I rule over Oppland in Norway. I have now come into my inheritance. But what is the name of those who have come here?"

They told him. Halfdan said, "I will offer you two choices, like other vikings. You may give up your money, ship, and weapons, but go free on land."

Njorfi answered, "That seems a hard choice. Instead, I will choose to defend my wealth and fall as a warrior should, if that is my fate, rather than flee, penniless and disgraced, even though you have greater forces and more and larger ships."

Viking said, "I will not treat you so basely and attack you with more ships than you have. Five of our ships will stay behind here."

Njorfi said, "That is spoken like a true warrior."

Then they prepared for combat, and began the battle and fought around the prows of their ships. There was the most furious fight, because Njorfi fought with the greatest daring, but the sworn brothers advanced fiercely. They fought for three days. Men couldn't tell which side would win.

Viking said, "Is there much wealth on your ships?"

Njorfi said that there wasn't—"because where we have raided this summer, the farmers ran away, carrying their own money. For that reason, our wealth has diminished."

"This seems foolish to me", said Viking, "to fight for nothing but reputation and spill the blood of many men. Would you prefer that we enter into fellowship with you?"[26]

"It would be good for me to establish a fellowship with you", said Njorfi, "although you are not born of kings. I know that your father was a jarl and a renowned man. I will bind myself to you in sworn brotherhood, on condition that you are called a jarl and I am called a king—the titles that we two were born with—whether we are in my kingdom or elsewhere."

Halfdan stood silently next to where they were talking. Viking asked why he was so reserved. Halfdan said, "I think it may be good for you to agree to this. But it wouldn't surprise me if you feel certain pressure from some of Njorfi's near relations. I will take no part in this, neither to hold you back nor to encourage you."

This was done: Njorfi and Viking made peace and swore an oath of brotherhood, according to the stated terms. They raided throughout the summer and gained much wealth, and they separated in the fall. Njorfi sailed to Norway, and Viking sailed to Sweden. Halfdan was on the journey with him.

But when Viking had not been home long, Hunvor became sick and breathed her last. They had one son after them, who was named Hring. He grew up in Sweden until he came of age and became a king there. He didn't live long, but many men are descended from him. But the sworn brothers went on raids every summer and became famous and gathered a multitude of ships, so that they had forty ships.

CHAPTER VIII

There is this to say about Ingjald Snout: He gathered a huge host and searched for the sworn brothers, Viking and Halfdan. One summer they met in the east Baltic. Ingjald had forty ships. The battle began. They fought so hard that it wasn't clear which of the two would win. At last, Viking managed to board Ingjald's dragon-ship, with Njorfi and Halfdan right behind him. They cleared a path furiously, killing one man after another. Ingjald rushed to the rear of the warship, and he had a great thrusting-spear to fight with. The sworn brothers now attacked Ingjald, and for the entire length of the day, they didn't land a wound on him. When it seemed that Ingjald was hard-pressed, he leaped over the side. Njorfi and Halfdan leaped after him, and each swam as hard as he could.

Viking didn't stop until he had killed every man on the dragon-ship. Then he jumped into a boat and rowed to shore.

Ingjald swam until he reached land. Then Halfdan and Njorfi came forward through the surf. Ingjald seized a stone and threw it at Halfdan, but he ducked under the water. Njorfi reached land, and so did Halfdan at another spot. Then they attacked Ingjald furiously. When that had gone on for a long time, they heard a great commotion. They looked for the place where the noise came from—but when they looked back, Ingjald had disappeared. In his place there was a horrible boar that left nothing undamaged. It attacked them, so that they could do nothing but defend themselves. When that had gone on for some time, the boar turned on Halfdan and bit the entire calf of his left leg. At that moment Viking came at him and struck in the middle of the boar's bristles, so that he split his back in two. They saw that Ingjald lay there dead. They took fire and burned him until nothing remained but cold ashes.

Now they went to their ships and bandaged Halfdan's wound. After that they sailed away, northward to the islands that are called Thruma[27]. There the man named Refil, son of Maefil the sea-king[28], was the ruler. He had a daughter named Finna. She was the loveliest of women and the most accomplished in all respects. Halfdan asked for her hand in marriage, and with King Njorfi's help and Viking's boldness, he got permission to marry her.

Then the sworn brothers left off their raiding. King Njorfi settled down in his kingdom with them. Viking settled down there and became the king's jarl, but Halfdan became a powerful hersir[29] and settled at the farm that was called Vagar.[30] There was a high mountain pass between him and the land which Jarl Viking ruled. They held on to their friendship while they lived, but there was less friendship between Halfdan and Njorfi.

CHAPTER IX

The king who ruled over Fjordane was named Olaf. He was the son of Eystein the brother of Onund, the father of Ingjald Bad-Ruler.[31] All of them were untrustworthy and difficult to deal with. He had a daughter who was named Bryngerd. Njorfi married her and kept her with him and had nine sons with her. Jokul was the oldest, the next was

Olaf, and then there were Grim, Feitir, Teit, Tyrfing, Bjorn, Geir, Grani and Toki. They were all promising men, yet Jokul was far ahead of them in all accomplishments. He was such an arrogant man that he thought no one could equal him. Olaf was next to him in all sports, but unruly and overbearing in every way, and full of injustice. So might one call all the brothers, and they were powerful men.

Viking also had nine sons. Thorstein was the name of his oldest son; the next was Thorir, and then there were Finn, Ulf, Stein, Hromund, Finnbogi, Eystein and Thorgeir. They were promising men and great men at sports, but Thorstein was above them in all respects. He was the biggest and the strongest, well-liked and a steadfast friend, trusty and true in all respects, long-suffering in all hardships—but he fiercely repaid ill treatment. If he was insulted, men could hardly tell from day to day whether he took it well or badly—but much later, he would behave as if the insult were fresh.

Thorir was impatient and the most eager man. He swelled with rage if harm or insult was done to him. And he wasn't afraid of consequences, no matter whom he might have to deal with or what might follow, and he did everything which entered his head to do. Of all men, he was the most agile in all sports and the strongest. He stood next to Thorstein, his brother.

These young men all grew up together in the kingdom.

On the mountain pass that ran between the homes of Viking and Halfdan, there was a chasm, amazingly deep. It was thirty ells across the chasm at its narrowest point. No men could get over it, and for that reason there was no passage over that mountain. King Njorfi and Jarl Viking and Halfdan had tested that, when they went to leap over the chasm. Viking made it in full armor, but Njorfi had dressed as lightly as possible. Halfdan only made it because Viking helped him over.

Now they all stayed quietly for a long time. The friendship of Jarl Viking and King Njorfi never waned.

CHAPTER X

Njorfi and Viking grew older, and their sons began to grow much. Jokul became a most arrogant man, unruly in every way. Njorfi's sons and Viking's sons were nearly the same age. At the time this saga tells of, the youngest sons were twelve years old, and Thorstein and Jokul were twenty. Njorfi's sons and Viking's sons played games together, and Viking's sons didn't get the worst of it. The king's sons' great pride vexed them over this. Jokul was the most impetuous, in this as in everything else. It was obvious that Thorstein was holding himself back in everything. Thorstein wasn't to be blamed for that; he far excelled his brothers and everyone else that men knew of. Jarl Viking had warned his sons that they should not contend with the king's sons over any game; instead, they should save their strength and energy.

One day, the king's sons and Viking's sons were playing *knattleikr*.[32] The sons of Njorfi were playing most vigorously. Thorstein was holding back, as he usually did. He was paired off against Jokul, and Olaf was paired against Thorir, and so each had been assigned a competitor of his own age. The game went on all day.

It so happened that Thorir hit the ball downwards so hard that it bounced over Olaf's head and landed far away. Olaf was enraged that Thorir seemed to be making fun of him. He looked for the ball. But when he came back, the players were parting, intending to go home. Olaf swung his bat at Thorir, but when Thorir saw that, he ducked under the blow, and the bat struck his head and broke the skin. Thorstein and the others rushed between them and separated them.

Jokul said, "You won't think this is a great matter, though Thorir got a bump on his head."

Thorir turned red at Jokul's words, and with that, they parted.

Then Thorir said, "I've left my gloves behind. Jokul will call me a coward if I don't dare look for them."

Thorstein said, "That doesn't seem like a good idea to me, for you and Olaf to encounter each other."

"I will go, as I've done before," said Thorir, "because they've gone home."

Thorir then went back quickly, and when he returned to the ball field, they had all left. Then Thorir went on, and came to the king's hall. At the very same moment, the king's sons came home to the hall and were standing by the walls. Thorir turned on Olaf and stabbed him in the belly with a spear, so that it went right through him. He turned and left, and they couldn't catch him. They raged over the dead body of Olaf, but Thorir traveled until he found his brothers.

Thorstein asked, "Why is there blood on your spear, brother?"

Thorir said, "Because I don't know whether Olaf might have gotten a scratch from the point."

"You must mean that he is dead," said Thorstein.

"It seems to me that it may be," said Thorir, "that, although Jokul may be a more accomplished man than most, he won't manage to heal his brother Olaf."

"This is a bad thing that has happened," said Thorstein, "because I know that my father won't like it."

And when they came home, Jarl Viking was outside, and he was very stern. He said, "So it happened with you, Thorir, just as I was afraid of—that you would be the most luckless of all my sons. It now seems that you have shown this, since you have become the slayer of the king's own son."

Thorir replied, "It's now time to help your son, father, though he may have come to ruin through misfortune. You have enough tricks that can help him—I think you have shown this, since you knew about the fight with Olaf ahead of time, and no one told you that."

Viking said, "I will not go so far to save Thorir's life as to break my oath, because King Njorfi and I have both sworn that each of us must be true and loyal, both privately and in public. I have held to that oath in every way. I will not be a worse man than he now, and be hostile to him, for there was a time when King Njorfi was no less beloved to me than my sons. And it goes without saying that I will give no help to Thorir. He must go away and never come before my eyes."

Thorstein said, "Why shouldn't we brothers all go away, since we won't be parted from Thorir? The same fate will befall both of us."

"You must decide, my son," said the jarl, "but it seems to me that Thorir's lack of luck must be great, if it causes me to lose all my sons, and along with that my friendship with the king, who is the better man in all respects—and also to lose my life, though in this case it's not worth much. But one thing gladdens me: no one will be able to stand on your scalp,[33] though you will have a narrow escape, and you will suffer all that on account of Thorir, though he will suffer some harm on account of his manliness. Now here is a sword which I will give you, Thorstein my son, which is called Angrvadil, and victory has always gone with it. My father took it from the dead Bjorn Bluetooth. I have no more weapons of any quality, aside from an old pike that I took from Harek Ironskull, and I know that it can't be wielded by any human. Now if you want to go away, Thorstein my son, I will give you this advice: go up to the lake called Vänern. There will be a boat in a boatshed which I own. Take the boat to the island that lies in the water. There will be enough supplies and clothes in a hut there to last you all for twelve months. Take good care of the boat, for there are no more ships in the vicinity."

Then the father and sons separated. They all had good clothes and armor, which their father had given them before this had happened. Thorstein went with his brothers, until they found the boat, rowed to the island and found the hut. There was plenty of everything that they needed, and they stayed there quietly.

CHAPTER XI

Now it is time to tell of how Jokul and his brothers told their father about Olaf's killing—"and there is nothing else to do", said Jokul, "but summon our forces, go to Viking's home and burn him and all his sons in his house, and yet this would hardly be full vengeance for Olaf."

Njorfi said, "I forbid outright that any harm be done to Viking. I know that it was not his intent to take my son's life. All of them are innocent, except for Thorir. And Viking and I have sworn an oath of brotherhood. He has held to that oath perfectly, and I will not offer him any violence. Even if Thorir should be killed, and Viking's grief be increased, I think that it would not be redress for Olaf's death."

Jokul got no help in this matter from his father. Olaf was laid in a burial mound, according to the old custom. Jokul then began to maintain a company of men. King Njorfi began to grow very old, so that Jokul took on most of the defense of the land.

One day, two men came before Njorfi. Both were wearing dark blue cloaks[34] with cowls. They greeted the king. The king asked them their names. One gave his name as Gautan, and the other was Ogautan.[35] They asked the king for lodging over the winter.

The king said, "You look evil to me. I will not receive you."

Jokul said, "Do you two know any kinds of skills?"

Ogautan said, "We know little of those, but yet we two know more than we've been told."

"Then it seems best," said Jokul, "for you to join my band and stay with me." So it was done. Jokul treated them well.

The news had gone as far as the king's hall that Viking had sent his sons away. Jokul didn't want to believe it, and went to Viking's house with many men. Viking asked what he wanted. Jokul asked what he knew about that wicked man Thorir. Viking said that he had sent them away and that they weren't there. Jokul asked to search his quarters. Viking allowed that at once, but he said that the king would not have imagined that he would be deceived. They ransacked the house and found nothing, as might be expected, and with matters as they stood, they went home. It seemed a shame to Jokul that he had heard nothing about the brothers.

Then Jokul said to Gautan and Ogautan, "Won't you use your skills to find out where the brothers are staying?"

"Probably not," said Ogautan. "You must get a house for us brothers to sleep in, and no one must come there but you, and not before three days have passed." Jokul had this done, and they were given a bower to sleep in. Jokul made a strict rule that if anyone called on them, he would lose nothing less than his life.[36]

Early on the appointed day, Jokul entered the brothers' bower. Ogautan said, "You are impatient, Jokul, since I have just now awakened. Still, I can tell you about the sons of Viking. You must know where that lake is that's called Vänern. There is an island standing in it, with a hut. Viking's sons are there."

Jokul said, "If this is as you say, then I see no hope that they may be caught."

Ogautan said, "You seem like a motherless child to me in every way, and I don't suppose that you accomplish much by yourself. Now I will tell you," said Ogautan, "that I have a bag called a wind-bag.[37] If I shake it, storms and winds blow from it, with such great frost and cold that within three nights there will be such thick ice on the water that we can ride horses on it if we want."

"It's truly said that you are a very crafty man," said Jokul. "This is the only way that we can get to the island, because there are no ships except for those on the sea-coast, and they can't be portaged for such a long distance."

After that, Ogautan took his bag and shook it. Out of it came dreadful weather with snowstorms and frost, so that no one could go outside, and people thought it was uncanny. And after three nights had passed, every lake and fjord was frozen over.

Jokul summoned his men; there were thirty all together. King Njorfi was not on this journey, for he had a foreboding that his grief would increase and not decrease: "I will lose most of my sons on this journey, and many other men. It would have been better, as I wished from the beginning, if we had reached a settlement with Thorir and had friendship with Jarl Viking and his sons."

CHAPTER XII

Now Jokul got ready, with thirty men and Gautan and Ogautan as well. That morning, Thorstein woke up in his hut and said, "Are you awake, Thorir?"

"I'm awake", he said, "but I was sleeping up to now."

Thorstein said, "I want us to get ready to leave the hut, because I know that Jokul will come here today with many men."

"I don't believe that," said Thorir, "and I want to stay at home. What signs of this do you have?"

"I dreamed," said Thorstein, "that thirty wolves were running towards this place, and there were seven bears and an eighth bear with red cheeks, and he was large and fearsome. There were also two vixens. They ran ahead of the company and were quite hideous, and they seemed the most disgusting to me. The wolves attacked us all, and it seemed to me that at last they tore apart all my brothers except for you alone, and yet you fell. It seemed to me that we killed many of the bears, and I killed all the wolves and the smaller vixen, and then I fell."

"What do you suppose your dream means?" said Thorir.

"I suppose," said Thorstein, "that the huge red-cheeked bear is Jokul's fetch[38], and the other bears are the fetches of his brothers, and as many wolves must have appeared to me as the men who will be with them, because their minds will be wolfish towards us. There were also two vixens. I don't know the men who must have those fetches. I suppose that they have just recently come to Jokul, and will be hateful to most men. Now I have told you what I think, and our encounter will go as it appeared to me in the dream. I want us to save ourselves from danger."

"I don't suppose that this is anything other than a nightmare and a foreboding," said Thorir, "although it wouldn't be boring if we were to put ourselves to the test."

"It doesn't seem that way to me," Thorstein replied, "and I believe that this is meant to be an unfair contest. I want us to get ready to leave."

Thorir replied that he didn't want to, and that was that. Thorstein stood up and took his weapons, and so did all his brothers. Thorir was the slowest.

At the same moment that they had armed themselves, Jokul came at them with his men. There were two doors in the hut. Thorstein defended one door with three of his brothers, and Thorir defended the other with four other men. The brothers defended themselves staunchly, but Jokul attacked so savagely at the doors that Thorir was defending, that three of Thorir's brothers fell, and one retreated from the doors to where Thorstein was. Then Thorir alone defended the doors for a little while, and by no means would he retreat. He burst out of the doors and came out onto the ice next to the invaders. They formed a ring around him, but he defended himself excellently.

When Thorstein saw that, he and his surviving brothers rushed out of the hut and onto the ice where Thorir was. Then there was a fierce fight. Thorstein and Thorir struck mighty blows. At last all of Thorstein's brothers had fallen except for Thorstein and Thorir, and all of Njorfi's sons had fallen except for Jokul and Grim. Thorstein was so terribly exhausted that he could hardly manage to stand up. He realized that he would fall. All of the other party had fallen except for Gautan and Ogautan. Thorir was both exhausted and wounded.

The night began to darken fast. Thorstein turned on Gautan and ran him through with Angrvadil, and then he fell among the slain. Three were left standing: Jokul, Grim and Ogautan. They searched for Thorstein among the slain. They thought that they found him, but it was Finn, Thorstein's brother, for they were so much alike that no one could tell them apart. Grim said that Thorstein was dead. Ogautan said that there should be no doubt, and cut off his head, and Finn didn't bleed because he was dead. Then they left there and came home.

King Njorfi heard how it had gone with them. The king said that their journey had accomplished nothing, and said that now he had received more harm than when he lost his son Olaf. Now seven of his sons and a great many more men were killed. Jokul now stayed home quietly.

CHAPTER XIII

The next thing to relate is that Thorstein lay among the slain and was unable to do anything from exhaustion, although he was only a little wounded. When the night had passed, he heard a wagon moving over the ice. Next he saw that a man was coming with the wagon. He recognized his father. And when he came to the slain, he cleared a way for himself and threw the bodies away from himself, and threw the king's sons harder than the others. He saw that all were dead except for Thorstein and Thorir. Then he asked whether they could say anything. Thorir said that he could, but Viking saw that his wounds were gaping. Thorstein said that he wasn't wounded, but very exhausted.

Viking took Thorir in his arms. It seemed to Thorstein that he picked him up with great strength, although he was very old. Thorstein got into the wagon himself and lay there with his weapons. Then Viking drove the wagon. The weather began to turn dark and cloudy, and it changed so quickly that in a very short while it seemed to Viking as if all the ice was disappearing. At precisely the same moment that they reached land, all the ice had turned to water.

Then Viking went home to his sleeping hut. There was a opening next to his bed, leading to an underground house, and he let them down into it. There was enough drink and food and clothing and everything needful. Viking healed his son Thorir, for he was a good healer. The other entrance to the underground house was in the forest. Viking warned his sons as strongly as possible that they should never go out of the house, because he said that as soon as Ogautan found out that they were alive, "we may immediately expect violence." Time now passed, until Thorir was completely healed.[39]

The news went around all the district that all the sons of Viking were now dead. Yet a certain rumor followed Ogautan, that it wasn't certain whether Thorir might be dead. Jokul asked him to seek out where Thorir was hiding, if he could find out. Ogautan pondered deeply, and yet was never any more certain about Thorir.

One day, Thorir said to Thorstein: "It seems stifling to me, here in this underground house. Now the weather is good, and I want us to go into the forest and enjoy ourselves."

"I don't want to do that," said Thorstein, "because then we would be disobeying our father's command."

"I said I would go," said Thorir. Thorstein had no desire to stay behind.

Then they went to the forest during the day and amused themselves. In the evening, when they meant to go home, they saw where a vixen was passing. She was nosing about in every direction and sniffing under every oak tree.

Thorir said, "What vile thing is coming here, kinsmen?"

"I'm not quite sure," said Thorstein. "I think that once I saw an animal like that one, but that was at night in the hut, before Jokul came, and my thought was that it was that bitch-skin[40] Ogautan."

He took his spear and threw it at the vixen, but she crept down into the earth. Now they went home to the underground house and didn't tell what had happened. A little later, Jarl Viking came there and said, "Now you two have done wrong. You have disobeyed my bidding and gone out of the house, and Ogautan has found out that you are here. I think we must expect that the brothers will come here soon with hostile intent."

CHAPTER XIV

A little later, Ogautan came to speak with Jokul and said, "It's quite true that I am your right hand and not your left."

"What is it now?" said Jokul.

"It's this," said Ogautan. "I have now found out that the brothers Thorir and Thorstein are alive, and are hiding with Viking."

"Then I will summon men and not relent until we have their lives," said Jokul.

Jokul got eighty men. There were thirty of the king's retainers among them; these were very well outfitted with clothes. They were ready at evening and intended to set out in the morning.

Two vagrant laborers had come there. One was named Vott, and the other was Thumal. When they had gone to bed in the evening, Vott said to Thumal, "Don't you think it's a good idea, brother, for us to get up and go to Viking and tell him Jokul's plan? Because I know that it will be the death of Viking if they come to him unawares—but we are bound to come to him and help him."

Thumal said, "Are you completely stupid? Don't you realize that the watchmen will detect us if we go out in the night, and then we'll be killed, and then we'll be of no help to Viking?"

"You always show that you've never amounted to anything," said Vott. "Even though you don't dare to budge, I will still go and warn Viking. Even if I get death, it seems worth the price to me if Viking should hold onto his life and his sons' lives, because he has often done good for me."

Vott stood up and dressed, and Thumal did so too, because he had no desire to stay behind. Then they went on their way, and came to Viking's home around midnight and awakened him from sleep. Vott told him that Jokul was expected to arrive there with a great many men. Viking said, "You have done well, my friend Vott, and you deserve a reward."

Viking called men together from the nearby settlements. He got thirty men. Then he went down into the underground house to his sons and told them what was about to happen.

Thorir said, "They will encounter resistance if they come. We will come up out of the underground house and fight them."

"You won't do that." said Viking. "First we will see how it goes with us. If things seem to me to have turned hopeless, I will go up on top of your underground house and make a great noise. Then you must help my men." Thorstein said that he would do so.

Then Viking went away. Day came, and he armed himself and all his men. He took the pike Harek's Gift in his hand. Everyone assumed that it would not be manageable on account of its weight, as old as Viking was. It astonished them that when Viking was in his armor, he seemed to be young once again. There was a high and wide stockade before Viking's farm, and that was the best stronghold. That was where he readied himself and his men. Weapons were given to Vott and Thumal.

CHAPTER XV

Now there is this to tell: Jokul got ready early in the morning with all his men, and didn't stop until he came to Viking's farm. Viking stood outside in front of the stockade and welcomed Jokul and all his men.

Jokul said, "You deserve something from us other than accepting your welcome. The reason we've come here is for you to surrender those wicked men, Thorstein and Thorir."

"I won't do that," said Viking, "but I won't deny that both of my sons are here. But I would give myself up rather than them. You may now attack, if you want to, and I and my men will defend."

They attacked fiercely, but Viking and his men defended themselves bravely. The fight went on for some time. Jokul attempted to get over the stockade and into the courtyard. Viking and his forces killed many men, but then all of his men began to fall.

Viking ran up above the underground house and pounded hard on his shield and made a great commotion. Thorir heard that, and told Thorstein that they should hurry—"but we must be late, because I believe that our father has fallen." Thorstein said that he was fully prepared, and when they came out, no men were left standing with Viking, except for Vott and Thumal and three other men. Viking was not yet wounded, but he was very weary.

As soon as the brothers came out, Thorstein turned on Jokul, and Thorir turned on Ogautan and his men. Twelve of King Njorfi's men attacked Viking and his men. Viking defended himself, but couldn't make any attacks against them. The man who was at their head was named Bjorn. In just a little while, Thorir killed all of Ogautan's followers and struck at Ogautan, but he plunged down into the earth, so that only the soles of his feet could be seen.

Then Thorstein attacked Jokul. Vott said, "It's good that you're testing each other to see who is braver, because Jokul has never been able to stand hearing that Thorstein is his equal in any respect." Now the battle was fiercest between Thorstein and Jokul. In the end, Jokul fell back from the stockade with many great wounds.

But when Jokul had retreated, Viking spared the lives of the surviving retainers of the king, and sent them away with fitting gifts and asked them to carry his friendly greetings to King Njorfi. And when Jokul came home, Ogautan had already come home. Jokul spoke sharply to him, for he had fled ahead of the others, but Ogautan said that he couldn't stand it there any longer— "and I might say that we've had to deal with trolls, rather than men." But Jokul told him that he'd said too much about it.

Somewhat later, King Njorfi's men came home, whom Viking had granted truce. They gave Viking's greetings to King Njorfi and told of all the favors which he had done for them. The king answered, "Viking is unlike most men, because of his gallantry and bravery. And I speak truly, Jokul my son, that I impose a ban on doing any violence to Viking from now on."

Jokul answered, "I don't like it that my brothers' killers are next to my property. And I can quickly say that Viking shall never have peace from me, nor his sons. I will never give up, until they are in Hel."

"I will find out which of us is more blessed with friendship," said the king, "because I will go and assist Viking's people, with all who will follow me. I think it is very important that you not slay Viking, because then I would have to do one of two things: either have you killed, and that would be ill spoken of, or break the oath that I swore to avenge Viking, if I should outlive him." And so he ended their conversation.

Viking came to talk with his sons, and he said, "I have no safe haven here to protect you from Jokul's power, but it's even more likely that some discord may come between me and King Njorfi, which I don't want."

Thorstein said, "What plan do you have for us?"

Viking said, "There is a man named Halfdan, and he rules over Vagar. That is on the other side of this mountain that stands here. He is an old friend and sworn brother of mine. I will send you there for protection. But there are many places along the way that are hard to pass: there are two hut-dwellers, each worse to deal with than the other. One is named Sam, and the other is Fullafli.[41] The name of Fullafli's dog is Gram, and he is little better to deal with than the occupant. Even if you escape both of them, it doesn't seem certain that you will reach Vagar, because a chasm, deep and wide, cuts across the mountain, which I know that no one has crossed except for us sworn-brothers. I think that Thorstein will most likely get across, but I'm not sure about Thorir."

A little later, the brothers made ready for the journey and took all their weapons. Viking gave Thorir the great pike. He gave a gold ring to his son Thorstein and asked him to give it to Halfdan as a token. "Thorir my son, be patient," said Viking, "even if Halfdan is wary with you, or pays no attention to you and your errand."

Then the father and sons parted. It seemed to Viking to be such a momentous event that tears ran down his cheeks. Viking watched them go, and said, "I will not see you again in my lifetime. Yet you will live to be an old man, son Thorstein, and become the most famous of men. Now travel safely and well."

The old man then turned homeward, but the brothers went up the mountain and came to a hut in the evening. There was a door, halfway shut. Thorir went to the door and pushed it in, and it took all his strength. When they entered the hut, they saw that many merchant's wares and all sorts of provisions were there. There was a large bed.

When the sun set, the hut's occupant came home, scowling. He said, "And here are come the wicked sons of Viking, Thorstein and Thorir, who have killed seven sons of Njorfi. Here there shall be an end to their wickedness, because it will be a small matter for me to lay you on the ground."

"Who is that who behaves so monstrously towards us?" said Thorir.

The hut-dweller said, "My name is Sam, son of Svart. Fullafli is the name of my brother, who rules the other hut."

Thorstein said, "I see that we brothers must be doomed to die, if you alone kill us both, so I'm not concerned about it if we two test each other. But Thorir will stand by."

At that, Sam rushed at Thorstein so quickly that Thorstein was overwhelmed, yet he didn't fall. Thorir rushed at him and stabbed the pike in his side and out the other. Sam dropped dead. They stayed there for the night and rested well, for there was plenty of food. They heated the hut, and didn't take any money away.

They left in the morning, and that evening they found another hut. This one was much larger. The door was shut. Thorir went to the door and tried to open it, and it wouldn't move. He went at it with all his strength, and it still wouldn't budge. Thorstein went to the door and pushed it open, and they went in. There was a pile of goods on one side, and a pile of firewood on the other. A large bed stood inside across the way, so that its size seemed immense to them. On the other side was a large space on the floor like a bed, round in shape. They decided that the dog Gram must lie there. Then they sat down and kindled a fire for themselves.

Long after nightfall, they heard heavy steps outside. Next the door was opened up. There came in a giant, amazingly large. He had a large bear tied up on his back, and a stringer of birds in front. He laid his burden down on the floor and said, "Bah! Here are the troublesome men, Viking's sons, who now have become the worst men in the land through their wickedness. How did you escape the clutches of my brother Sam?"

"We got away in such a way," said Thorstein, "that Sam lies dead behind us."

"You betrayed him in his sleep," said Fullafli.

"That wasn't it," said Thorstein, "we fought, and my brother Thorir killed him."

"I will not act shamefully to you tonight," said Fullafli. "You shall wait until morning, and have food as you like."[42]

Then the hut-dweller cut up the game he had caught and took a table and set out food. They all began to eat. After that they all went to sleep. The two brothers lay together in their shaggy cloaks. The dog didn't like it when they walked past him. Neither tried to deceive the other.

In the morning both the brothers and Fullafli got up early. Then Fullafli said, "Now Thorstein will try himself against me, and Thorir against my dog in another place."

"You must decide this," said Thorstein.

Then they went outside, into the field in front of the hut. At once the dog leaped at Thorir with his jaws gaping, and they had the hardest fight, because the dog beat away every blow with his tail—but if Thorir struck with the pike, the dog bit it and knocked every strike away from himself. They attacked each other for three hours, and Thorir didn't wound him. Then in an instant, Gram sprang at Thorir and gripped him by the calf and bit off a piece. At that moment, Thorir stabbed the dog with the pike and pinned him to the ground, and Gram died soon after.

There is to tell about Fullafli: he had a huge blade in his hand, and Thorstein had his own sword. They had a fight both hard and long, because Fullafli struck with powerful blows. But because Angrvadil bit armor as well as flesh, Fullafli fell dead, but Thorstein wasn't wounded.

CHAPTER XVI

Now the brothers got ready to leave, and went their way until they came to the great chasm. It looked to Thorstein to be hard to get over. Yet he took a running jump and leaped over the chasm, with Thorir right behind him. At the same instant that Thorstein turned back towards the chasm's edge, Thorir had landed on the edge and was about to fall backwards. At that moment, Thorstein got a grip on him and pulled him up over the edge of the chasm.

Thorstein said, "You always show how hot-headed you are, brother, and you did it again, because you might have known that falling into the chasm would be sudden death."

"That didn't happen," said Thorir, "and once again, I benefitted from you, as I often have before."

Now they went on their way until they came to a great river, both deep and fast. Thorstein asked that they search for a place where it could be forded. Right then Thorir waded out into the river, and when he had gone a short distance from the shore, he couldn't touch bottom and had to exert himself by swimming. Thorstein had no desire to stay on land, and he jumped out into the river after him. They came onto land and wrung out their clothes. But while they were at that, the frost became so great that their clothes froze and became like stone, and they could not get into them. Then there came a great blizzard, and the men supposed that Ogautan must have caused this weather.

Thorstein asked Thorir what he advised. "It seems advisable to me," said Thorir, "that we stick our clothes down in the river, because they will loosen up quickly in cold water." They did so, and with this trick, they got into their clothes.

They went on their way until they came to the dwelling at Vagar. The door was locked, and they couldn't get in. It was evening. They pounded at the doors for a long time, and no one came. A beam twenty ells long lay in the yard. They picked it up and carried it up onto the house and rode on it, so that every one of the rafters began to creak. All the people in the house were so afraid that each one rushed into his own corner.[43]

Halfdan then went to the door and came out into the courtyard. The brothers went up to him and greeted him. Halfdan answered them coldly, but he asked them their names. They gave their names and said that they were the sons of Jarl Viking, saying that he sent him greetings.

Halfdan said, "I can't claim sworn-brotherhood with you. I think that many keep it passably well, but no better. It seems as though you don't let it extend to the rest of the family, since you have killed almost all of the sons of King Njorfi. But you may come inside and stay here for the night, if you wish."

He turned on his heel and went inside, and they followed. They came into the common room. There were few people there. No one took the clothes off them. They sat there like that through the evening, until it was time to go to bed. Then a trough was set on the table before them, with porridge in it, and also a spoon at each end. Thorir picked it up and ate the porridge. Thorstein said, "You have less pride than you ought to." He picked up the trough and threw it out onto the floor, so that it broke in pieces. Then people went to bed. The brothers had no bed, and they got no sleep that night.

They got up early in the morning and prepared for their journey. And when they came out before the doors, the man of the house came up and said, "What did you say yesterday—whose sons did you say that you were?"

Thorir said, "What more do you want to know than what we already told you—that we were the sons of Jarl Viking?"

Thorstein said, "Here is a gold ring that he asked me to give you."

Thorir said, "I suppose that whoever shows any of the ring to him will be the worse for it."

Thorstein said, "Don't be so peevish, brother. Here is the gold as a token that you may receive us, so that we may have refuge here with you."

Halfdan accepted the gold and was happy with it, and said, "Why would I not welcome you and do everything good that I can for you? I owe you that for the sake of my friend Viking. You seem to me to be blessed with good luck."

Thorir said, "It's true what they say: 'it's good to have two mouths, each with its own voice'. You received us differently yesterday evening, when we came here. You must be the greatest coward, and you are cunning in every way."

Thorstein said, "We must have patience with my brother, Halfdan, even though he speaks ill of you, because he is reckless in words and deeds."

"I've heard that," said Halfdan. "You are the most able man, but Thorir is rash and reckless—yet I think that you will be more high-minded in everything."

They went inside, and their clothes were taken off and they were given the best hospitality. They stayed there through the winter in great favor.

When the spring days had come, Thorstein said to Halfdan, "Now we two will set out on a journey away from here."

"What do you most want to do?" said Halfdan.

"I want you to give me a ship," said Thorstein, "and men in it. I will go raiding and get some money for myself." Halfdan said that it should be so.

They set out towards the lands to the south. There, two ships which his father had sent to Thorstein came to meet him, laden with men and good weapons. Thorstein sent back the ship which Halfdan had given him, and the men with it, and each of the brothers captained his own ship. They raided far and wide over the summer, and they gained much wealth and glory.

In the autumn they came to a certain island. A farmer named Grim ruled over it. He invited them to stay there through the winter, and they accepted. Grim was married and had one daughter, named Thora. She was fully grown and beautiful in appearance. Thorir had his mind set on her, and told his brother Thorstein that he wanted to have her for his wife. Thorstein discussed the matter with the farmer Grim. Grim denied it outright.

Thorstein said, "Then I challenge you to a duel, and whichever of us wins the duel will decide your daughter's fate."

Grim said that it was agreed. The next day they took a cloak and laid it under their feet,[44] and fought most manfully, and separated at evening. Neither one was wounded. They fought for a second day and a third, and it went the same way.

That same day, Thorir asked the farmer's daughter what would cause Grim to be defeated. She said that there was one stone on the forefront of his helmet. As long as the stone was not near him, this would ensure that he could not win. Thorir told this to Thorstein, and on the fourth day that they fought, Thorstein threw away his sword and gripped the helmet with both hands, so hard that the straps broke. A moment later he attacked Grim, and Grim realized the odds against him. Thorstein subdued him and spared his life.

Then Grim asked who had given him the advice to take the helmet. Thorstein said that Thora had told it to Thorir.

"Then she wants to be married," said Grim. "So be it."

It was agreed that Thorir should marry Thora. And in spring, Thorstein set out on his raiding, but Thorir stayed behind. Thorir and Thora came to love each other well. They had one son who was named Harald. He took the spear-pike after his father. From it he got his name, and was called Harald Pike.[45]

CHAPTER XVII

There was a king named Skati. He was the son of Eirik, the son of Myndil, the son of Meitalf. King Skati ruled over Sogn. He was married to a queen and had two children. His son was named Beli, the boldest of men. His daughter was named Ingibjorg. She was not in the kingdom at the time, because she had been put under a spell earlier.

Skati had been a berserk and the greatest raider, and had forced his way into ruling Sogn. Thorgrim was the name of the man in charge of his land's defenses. He was the mightiest champion and a great fighter, but only moderately trustworthy. There was strong friendship between Thorgrim and Beli the king's son. Beli was the most renowned man in all the land.

The story goes that when King Skati was very old and his children were both young, two raiders attacked his land. One was named Gautan, and the other was Ogautan. They caught the king completely by surprise and summoned him to battle, or else he would have to make them jarls and give up his land. King Skati had no troops to challenge them, although he preferred to die with honor rather than live with shame, and fall in his own kingdom rather than serve his enemies. He went to the battle, and had no more forces than his personal guard. Thorgrim got away with Beli the king's son, but Ingibjorg stayed behind in her bower.

King Skati fell before Ogautan, winning much glory, but his surviving men fled into the forest.

Ogautan now settled in the kingdom and had himself given the title of king. He asked Ingibjorg to marry him, but she flatly refused him and said that she would kill herself before she would marry her own father's killer, such a villain as Ogautan was—"for you are more like a fiend than a man."

Ogautan was angry with her and said, "I will pay you back for your harsh words. I lay this spell upon you, that you will be identical in size and appearance to my sister Skellinefja[46], and take on all of her nature, as much as you can bear; and that you shall live in that cave which lies along Deep River, and never escape from this enchantment until some well-born man comes forth and agrees to marry you, but never before I am dead. And my sister shall take on your appearance."

"I pronounce this," said Ingibjorg, "that you will enjoy this kingdom both poorly and briefly."[47]

The spells which Ogautan spoke came true, and so Ingibjorg was transformed. A little later, Beli the king's son and Thorgrim came back with many men in the middle of the night, and they set fire to the roof of the hall where the brothers were sleeping. They burned all of the men inside, except that the brothers took the "nether road" and so got away. They didn't stop until they had come to the household of King Njorfi. But Beli took his own kingdom and made himself king over it. Thorgrim was still the guardian of his lands.

CHAPTER XVIII

There was a king named William who ruled over Normandy[48], a wise and popular king. He had a daughter, who was named Olof, the most cultivated of women.

Now there is this to say about Jokul Njorfi's son: After the sons of Viking had gone away, he made Thorstein and Thorir outlaws throughout the length of his kingdom. King Njorfi did not agree with that, because he and Viking held to their friendship while they lived.

On one occasion, Ogautan came to speak with Jokul and asked whether he didn't want to marry. Jokul asked whether he had seen a woman who was an equal match for him. Ogautan said, "William of

Normandy has a daughter named Olof. I believe that your honor will increase if you make a match with her."

"Why shouldn't we try?" said Jokul.

They made ready for the trip, with sixty men, and they traveled to Normandy and met King William. He welcomed Jokul, because the name of his father Njorfi was known in all lands. Jokul began to press his suit for Olof's hand. Ogautan strongly supported his courtship, but the king left it up to his daughter.

When they had discussed it, thirty most valiant men came into the hall. The one who led them was the tallest and most handsome. He went before the king and greeted him. As soon as Ogautan saw these men, he went silent and his beard drooped, and he said to Jokul and his other men that they must not give their names while they were there in that land.

The king asked these great men to name themselves, and the leader said that he was named Beli and was the son of King Skati, who ruled in Sogn—"and my errand here is that I wish to ask for your daughter's hand."

The king said, "Jokul Njorfason has come here before you and asked for her. I will now resolve this: she may choose which one she will marry."

The king had Beli sit on his other side, and the best of feasts was held. When three nights had passed. they went out to the bower and asked the king's daughter whom she preferred to marry, Jokul or Beli. Soon it was easy to see that she preferred to marry Beli. At that, Ogautan threw a stick onto her lap, and she was so startled by it that she turned down Beli and went to marry Jokul.[49] Beli returned to his ships. There had already been a friendly agreement made between Jokul and Beli, so that some say that Beli must have taken money for the heads of the brothers Thorstein and Thorir. Although the king's daughter didn't want to marry him, Beli didn't try to force Jokul's hand, because it was her decision.

Beli went home to his kingdom. Jokul went home as soon as his wedding was over, and Ogautan went with him.

CHAPTER XIX

Now the story goes on that Thorstein headed home from his raiding and meant to go to the farmer Grim, because Thorir his brother was staying there on the island. Jokul had news of his journey. He told Ogautan, and asked him to try his skills and send a storm at Thorstein, so that he and all his men would be drowned. Ogautan said that he would try, however it might turn out. He then sent such a great sorcerous storm at Thorstein that his ship and every man on it were lost at sea. Thorstein held out long and well, but it turned out in the end that he became exhausted with swimming. He had come into the surf, but by then he was being dragged under. At that moment he saw that a large old woman was wading out to him, wearing a wrinkled blouse made of skins. It was long in the front and scanty in the back.[50] She was very gaunt and quite monstrous in appearance. She went to him and pulled him out of the sea and said, "Will you accept your life from me, Thorstein?"

He said, "How could I not want that? But what is your name?"

She said, "My name's not lacking, I'm called Skellinefja. But you must be willing to do something, for your life to be saved."

"What is that?" he said.

"To grant me the favor that I will ask of you," she said.

"You will ask for this one thing," said Thorstein, "that will go well for me. When will that be?"

"Not yet," she said.

Then she carried him to land, and he had then come onto that island which Grim had ruled over. She started to wrestle a bit with him, so that he might warm up. Then she parted from him, and each wished the other well. She went her own way, for she said that she had farther to go, but Thorstein went home to the farm. There was a happy reunion between the two brothers. Thorstein stayed there through the winter in great favor.

Now there is this to tell: when Jokul and Ogautan sailed home, on a certain day with good weather, a great darkness broke out above the ship, with such terrible biting frost that no man on the ship dared to turn his face into it. All the men on the ships pulled their clothes over their faces. But when the darkness passed, they saw Ogautan, hanging from the top of the mast, dead[51]. Jokul though that this was the greatest loss, and he sailed home to his kingdom and stayed there quietly.

Thorstein and Thorir prepared to set out early in the spring, meaning to visit the home of Viking their father. And when they came to Deep River, they had no warning that Jokul had come after them with thirty men. At once a battle broke out between them. Jokul was the most furious and so was Grim, his brother. Thorir and Thorstein defended themselves well. For a long time the brothers took no wounds. Not only was Thorstein a strong striker, but Angrvadil cut iron like cloth. Thorir defended himself most bravely, but he didn't have the pike, because he had left it at home. They attacked Grim and fought most boldly, and in the end Grim sank down to the ground, dead. By then Thorstein had killed nineteen men, but he was both exhausted and wounded, and so was Thorir. The brothers then turned back to back, and still defended themselves well. Jokul attacked them with eleven men and made such a fierce onslaught that Thorir fell. Then Thorstein defended himself manfully, until no more were left except for Jokul and three others.

Then Jokul stabbed at Thorstein and pierced him high up on his thigh. Since Jokul was strong and drove his thrust home, but Thorstein was very exhausted and was standing on the edge of the riverbank, he fell over the bank, but Jokul nimbly managed to stop himself from falling. Then Jokul set out for home and believed that he had killed Thorstein and Thorir. He stayed there quietly.

Now there is this to tell about how Thorstein fell over the bank. There was a tuft of grass where he landed, but he could not move because of his exhaustion and wounds, yet he remained conscious after his fall. Angrvadil was knocked out of his hand and fell into the river. Thorstein lay there, between Earth and Hel, and expected nothing but death for himself.

He hadn't lain there long when he saw that Skellinefja was coming. She was wearing her skin-blouse and was no prettier than before.[52] She came to where Thorstein was lying and said, "I don't believe you can clear the rocks out of your road, Thorstein. It seems that you're dying. Are you willing to grant me that favor that I bargained for with you before?"

Thorstein said, "I'm afraid that I can't do much now, as helpless as I am."

"This is the favor," she said, "that you agree to marry me. I will then try to heal you."

Thorstein said, "I don't know whether I can manage that, because you look monstrous to me."

"But you must make a choice," she said, "whether you would rather marry me, or lose your life and break the oath to grant me a favor, which you swore when I saved your life on Grim's island."

Thorstein said, "There's a lot of truth in that, and it's best to keep one's word. I will agree to marry you. You will be the most helpful person to me, but I would ask that you get my sword, so that I can carry it, if I survive."

She said that it would be done, and picked him up in her blouse and leaped up the bluff as if she were unencumbered, until a great cave was before them. She went inside it and bound Thorstein's wounds, and laid him in a soft bed. Within seven nights he was completely healed.

One day Skellinefja was away from the cave, and in the evening she came back with the sword, and it was dripping wet. She gave it to Thorstein and said, "Now I have given you your life twice, and given you back your sword, which you value the most greatly. The fourth thing, which is the greatest benefit to both of us, is that I hanged Ogautan. But you have fully rewarded me for that, because you have brought me out of the spell which Ogautan laid on me. My name is Ingibjorg, the daughter of King Skati and the sister of Beli, and if any well-born man agreed to marry me, that would release me from my bondage. You did this, and I am now free from my bondage. You must now make ready to leave the cave and go forward according to my plan. You will find my brother Beli with five men. Thorgrim Seal, the guardian of his lands, will be there with him. They have taken money from Jokul for your head. They will start a fight with you. I don't care if you kill Thorgrim and his companions, but spare the life of Beli, my brother. I want you to become sworn brothers. And if you have it in mind to marry me, go home to Sogn with him and ask for me, and I will be there ahead of you. It may be that I will appear differently to you from what you see now."

Now they parted. When Thorstein had gone a short way, Beli came after him with five men in all. When they met, Thorgrim said, "That is well, Thorstein, that we have found each other. Now we will earn the price that Jokul has put on your head."

"I think it's possible that you'll lose the money, and your life," said Thorstein.

CHAPTER XX

Now there is this to tell: they attacked Thorstein, but he defended himself well and manfully, and in the end Thorgrim and three of his companions fell. Then Thorstein and Beli fought again. Thorstein defended himself but didn't want to wound Beli, but Beli attacked him until Thorstein grabbed him and set him down next to him and said, "I have the advantage of you, but I will grant you your life, and along with it, I will have us become sworn brothers. You shall be king, and I your hersir. I will also ask to marry Ingibjorg, your sister, and to have estates in Sogn as her dowry."

"That isn't easy," said Beli, "because my sister has gone away, and no one knows what has become of her."

"It may be," said Thorstein, "that she has come back."

"I don't see that she could get a more valiant man than you," said Beli, "and I will give you all that you ask for."

They bound themselves by swearing oaths, and went home to Sogn. Beli suddenly realized that his sister had come back, in the same bloom of youth as she had had before. Thorstein made his suit and asked for the hand of Ingibjorg. The marriage was agreed upon. She had as her dowry those estates which lay on the other side of the fjord. The farm that Thorstein governed was called Framnes, and the one that Beli had was Syrstrond.

Beli and Thorstein set out raiding in the summer and had five ships. They raided widely in the summer and gained much wealth, and sailed home in the autumn with seven ships.

The next summer they set out raiding and didn't get much wealth, because all the vikings avoided them. And when they came to the skerries that are called the Göteborg Islands, they reached harbor in the evening. Thorstein and Beli landed and went across the cape where their ships lay. But when they came over the cape, they saw twelve ships, covered over with black tents. They saw a tent on land, with smoke coming from it, and they realized that those must be the ship's cooks. They threw disguises over themselves and went there, and when they came to the tent doors, they blocked both doors, so that the smoke wasn't able to come out. The ones who were preparing food spoke harshly and asked what kind of beggars they were, who were so deceitful that they wanted to burn them or smother them inside. They spoke crudely and answered with hollow voices, and said that they wanted to get food for themselves—"who is the bold one who captains this fleet that's anchored by this land?"

"You must be stupid old men," they said, "if you haven't heard about Ufi, who is called Slysa-Ufi,[53] son of Herbrand the Big-Headed. He is the brother of Otunfaxi.[54] I know of no one more famous under the sun than they."

"Well said," said Thorstein. A little later they went away to their own men.

Early in the morning they got ready and rowed out in front of the cape. They shouted out their battle-cry. The others quickly prepared themselves and took up their weapons, and a fierce battle began. Ufi had more men, and he himself was the hardiest. They fought for so long that no one could tell which side was winning.

On the third day, Thorstein boarded the dragon-ship that Slysa-Ufi captained, and Beli was right behind him. They boldly cleared a path before them and killed every man standing before the sail. Then Ufi charged down from the afterdeck at Beli, and they traded blows for a while. Beli suffered wounds, because Ufi was both skilled with weapons and a powerful striker.

At that moment, Thorstein came up with Angrvadil and swung at Ufi. That blow struck him on his helmet and cleaved all of the man's body and armor lengthwise, and the sword cut so deeply into the mast-block that both edges were buried. Beli said, "That blow of yours, sworn-brother, will be praised while the Northlands are inhabited."

After that, they offered the vikings two options: to surrender and save their lives, or fight a battle against them. The vikings preferred to accept life from them. The sworn brothers granted them all a truce, because the vikings wanted to accept it willingly. They took much booty. They anchored there for three nights and healed their own men, and sailed home in the autumn.

CHAPTER XXI

In the spring the sworn brothers prepared to leave their home, and they had fifteen ships. Beli sailed the dragon-ship which Slysa-Ufi had had. It was a good possession, with carved beaks and engraving and much gilding. King Beli was allotted the dragon-ship because it was the best possession among the plunder which they got from Ufi, and their custom was that Beli always took the costly things that they plundered.

No other ship seemed better than that dragon-ship, aside from Ellidi, which Ufi's brother Otunfaxi had. They had inherited these ships from Herbrand their father, and Ellidi was better because it had a favorable wind wherever Otunfaxi might want to sail. It could almost understand human speech. Otunfaxi had been allotted Ellidi rather than Ufi, because Ufi had had the misfortune of killing his father and mother, and it seemed to Otunfaxi that he had forfeited his own inheritance, if justice were done. Otunfaxi was foremost of the brothers because of his strength and size and sorcery.

Now the sworn brothers set out on raids and harried widely in the eastern realms, and found few vikings, because everyone who heard of their coming fled from them. There were no more celebrated men for raiding than Thorstein and Beli.

One day, they anchored at a certain promontory. The sworn brothers saw that on the other side, there lay twelve ships at anchor under the cape, all of them large. They rowed swiftly towards the ships and asked who was in charge of this host. A man stood up by the mast and said, "I am called Angantyr, son of Hermund the jarl of Gautland."

"You are a promising man," said Thorstein, "but how old are you?"

He answered, "I am nineteen years old now."

"Which would you prefer," said Beli, "to give up your ships and wealth, or have a battle with us?"

"The less equal the choices, the easier it is to choose,"[55] said Angantyr. "I would rather defend my wealth, and die bravely if this is my fate."

"Then prepare yourself for us to attack you," said Beli

Both sides prepared themselves and broke out their weapons. Thorstein said to Beli, "It is hardly a warrior's deed to attack them with fifteen ships, when they have no more than twelve."

"Why not let three of our ships stay here?" said Beli. They did so.

There was a fierce battle. Angantyr's forces were so hardy that it seemed to Beli and Thorstein that they had never been in a greater trial. They fought that day till evening, so that no one could decide which of the two would win.

On the second day they prepared for battle. Then Angantyr said, "I think that it's best for us, King Beli, not to waste our men's lives any longer. The two of us should fight a duel. Let the one who defeats the other be the victor."

Beli agreed to this. They went on land and spread a cloak under their feet and fought valiantly, until Beli was tired and there were wounds on him. Thorstein realized that Beli couldn't win against Angantyr, and things had come to the point that Beli was exhausted and completely on his last legs. Thorstein said, "I think it advisable, Angantyr, for you to break off the fight, because I see that Beli is overcome with exhaustion. I don't want to be so mean as to behave shamefully towards you, but I want to assist him. And it would happen, if you were to slay him, that I would challenge you to a duel, and I suppose there is no less difference between me and you than there is between you and Beli. I would kill you in the duel, and that would be a great loss if both of you perished. Now I will offer you this choice: if you spare Beli's life, the two of us will swear brotherhood with you."

Angantyr said, "That seems a fair offer, that Beli and I will become sworn brothers. But I think it will benefit me all the more if I become your sworn brother."

The brotherhood was then bound by the speaking of oaths. They let their blood flow from the palms of their hands, and went beneath a loop of turf[56], and swore the oath that each one had to avenge the others, if any of them were slain with weapons.

Then they assembled their forces. Two ships from each side had lost all their crews. They healed their men who were wounded. After that, they sailed away from there with twenty-three ships, and sailed for home in the autumn, and stayed there quietly in the winter with much honor. No men now seemed more famous for their raiding than the sworn brothers.

CHAPTER XXII

Now when spring came, the sworn brothers prepared to leave home, and they had thirty ships. They set their course for the eastern realms and raided there, around Sweden and all the eastern Baltic Sea. Their raids went well. As was their custom, they killed vikings and robbers wherever they could catch them, but let farmers and merchants go in peace.[57]

Now the story moves to another place, where Otunfaxi found out about the fall of Ufi, his brother. That seemed to him to be a great loss. There is this to tell about him: he searched for the sworn brothers for three summers in a row.

Now there is this to tell: King Beli and his sworn brothers anchored one day at the skerries that are called the Brenni Islands.[58] They stayed there in an anchorage and prepared themselves well. Afterwards, the three sworn brothers went ashore and traveled until they came to a small farm. There stood a man before the doors, chopping wood. He was wearing a green tunic and was very fat. He greeted Thorstein by name.

Thorstein said, "We must not be equally good at recognizing faces. You greet me by name, but I don't remember seeing you. What is your name?"

"My name's not lacking," he said. "I am called Brennir, and I am the son of Vifil, the brother of Viking, your father. Vifil fathered me when he was out raiding, when he had his home near to Halogi. I have grown up here on the island and settled here since then. But, kinsman Thorstein, have you heard anything about the viking Otunfaxi?"

"I haven't," said Thorstein, "but what can you tell us about him?"

"This," said Brennir, "that he has searched for you for three years, and he is anchored here on the other side of the island, with all his fleet. He wants to avenge Slysa-Ufi, his brother. He has forty ships, all of them large. He is as big as a troll, and iron doesn't bite him."

"What do you advise?" said Thorstein.

"I have no advice to give you," said Brennir, "except that you should try to find the dwarf Sindri, because I know that he's on bad terms with him, and he won't be lacking in advice."

"Where can I expect to find him?" said Thorstein.

"He has a home on the island that lies just a short distance off the land, called Lesser Brenniey. He lives in a stone, and I think it's unlikely that you'll manage to find him. But this place is at your service tonight."

"One mustn't sit quietly before a battle," said Thorstein. Then they went to their ships.

Thorstein set out in his boat and rowed to the island. He went ashore alone. And when he came to a brook, he saw that two children were playing by the brook, a boy and a girl. Thorstein asked them their names. The boy gave his name as Herraud, and the girl was Herrid.

"I have lost my gold ring," she said. "I know that my father Sindri won't like that. I must expect punishment."

Thorstein said, "Here is a gold ring that I will give you."

She accepted the gold and was glad to have it—"and I will give this to my father. Can't I do something that would be helpful to you?"

"You can't," said Thorstein, "but bring your father here to talk with me. Let it be so that he gives me advice about the matter that concerns me."

"There's only one way to get that done," said Herrid, "and that's for Herraud my brother to do what I want, because Sindri indulges him in everything."

"You know that I follow you in every way," said Herraud.

Thorstein unbuckled his silver belt and gave it to him. An ornamented knife went with it. The boy said, "This is a fine gift. I will try with all my heart to see to it that your case goes forward. Wait here till my sister and I come back with him." Thorstein did so.

When a long time had passed, Sindri the dwarf came there, and the brother and sister with him. Sindri greeted Thorstein cheerfully and said, "What do you want of me, Thorstein?"

"What I want," said Thorstein, "is for you to advise me on how I can manage to defeat Otunfaxi the viking."

"I don't see a way for any human to beat Faxi," said Sindri. "He is much harder to deal with than anyone else. I want to discourage you from battling with him, because you would lose your men there, and the best thing for you is to sail away from these islands at night."

"That shall never be," said Thorstein. "Even if I knew in advance that I would lose my life, I would prefer that to fleeing without trying."

"I see that you are the greatest champion," said Sindri. "I would advise you to unload all your ships at night and bring your wealth onto land, but load the ships with logs and stones. Then get up early in the morning and come at them before they awake. You might be able to take them by surprise in their tents.[59] You need to do all this if you manage to get Faxi to give way at all, because I will tell you that not even the sword Angrvadil will bite him, and so much the less will any iron bite him. Here is a little knife which Herrid my daughter will give you as a reward for the ring. I suppose it might bite Otunfaxi, if you use it skillfully. Herraud, my son, will reward you for the belt in this way: you shall call on me by name if it seems to you that something is going wrong. We will part for now. Fare well and hale. I pronounce that my disir[60] shall go with you always."

Then Thorstein went to his boat and rowed back to his men. All through the night he made preparations and unloaded the wealth from his ships, and loaded stones in its place. And when that was done, the old man Brennir came over from the farm. He had a large club in his hand, all mounted with iron, and with huge iron spikes. It was so heavy that an average man could hardly lift it off the ground. Brennir said, "I want to give you this hand weapon, kinsman Thorstein. Only you will be able to wield it because of its weight, yet it will be rather light against Otunfaxi. I think it best that Angantyr should have the sword Angrvadil, and you should carry the club. Although the club may not be handy to carry, still it will deal harm to men. I would like to give you more help, kinsman, but I don't have the resources for that." Then he turned back up onto the land.

CHAPTER XXIII

Then they rowed out in front of the cape where they were stationed, and they could see where Otunfaxi lay at anchor with all his ships. At once they released a shower of flung stones, so hard and furious that they killed more than a hundred men before they awoke. But as soon as the men awoke, they put up a stiff defense. Then the battle was deadliest. Many of the sworn brothers' men fell, because one might say that Faxi shot arrows from every finger.[61] So it went until night. Ten of the sworn brothers' ships were emptied of men.

On the second day, they began fighting, and the slaughter was as great as on the first day. They constantly tried to board Faxi's ship, and they made a great slaughter every time, but they never made it onto the dragon-ship Ellidi, because of Faxi's defense and also because Ellidi had such high sides. In the evening all of the sworn brothers' ships were empty, except for the dragon-ship Ufi's Gift.

On both days, they saw one man come out onto each of two cliffs and shoot furiously at Faxi's ship. They saw the dwarf Sindri, and he hit a man with every arrow. Faxi suffered many losses from this. On the other cliff was Brennir, and he shot at the ships like a great archer. There was no protection when he let stones fly at the ships, and all the stones that he threw went to the bottom of the sea, sinking many of Faxi's ships. In the end, it happened that all of his ships were cleared, except for Ellidi.

That was at the time when nights were bright, and they battled all night. Thorstein tried to board the dragon-ship with Angantyr and Beli, and many men followed them onto Ellidi. Faxi rushed forward to meet the sworn brothers, Angantyr and Beli. They had a fierce exchange of blows. No iron weapons bit Faxi, but they had not fought long before both Angantyr and Beli were wounded. At that, Thorstein came at him and struck with the club as hard as he could against the side of Faxi's head, but Faxi never bowed down from that. Then Thorstein struck again, no less hard. The blow bothered Faxi, and he leaped over the side and into the water so that only the soles of his feet could be seen. Beli and Angantyr were both too astonished to follow him.

Thorstein at once leaped over the side and swam after the fleeing Faxi. Faxi's motion looked most like a whale swimming. This went on a long time, until Faxi came ashore. But the sworn brothers fought with the men who stayed behind, and didn't stop until they had killed everyone on the dragon-ship. Then they took the boat and rowed to land, where Faxi and Thorstein were.

Now that Faxi had come ashore, as Thorstein swam towards him, Faxi grasped a stone and threw it at Thorstein. But he dived under the water and swam out from under it, and there was a great crash when the stone landed. Faxi picked up a second and a third, and the same thing happened. And at that moment, the sworn brothers Angantyr and Beli came up. Thorstein had thrown the club back onto the ship when he jumped over the side, and Beli had picked up the club and come to where Otunfaxi was standing. He struck the back of his head with the club, from behind, and then struck again, and Angantyr pelted him with large stones.

Faxi's bald head now began to hurt very much, and he grew weary of being under their blows. He plunged from the cliff into the water. He swam out into the sea and Thorstein swam after him. When Faxi saw that, he turned to meet Thorstein, and they began grappling in the water. They had a huge wrestling match, and each dunked the other in the sea, yet Thorstein realized how much stronger Faxi was. Then it happened that Faxi dragged Thorstein to the bottom, keeping him from swimming. Thorstein realized that Faxi meant to bite his windpipe in two, and he said, "At what other time would I have more need for you than now, dwarf Sindri?"

With that, Thorstein became aware that something had gripped Faxi by the shoulders, so hard that the next thing was that he was down on the bottom, with Thorstein on top of him. Thorstein was very exhausted and battered from their struggle. He took the little knife that Sindri had given him, and he stabbed it just below Faxi's ribs, so that it sank up to the hilt. Then he tore all his belly open, right down to the intestines. Yet he found that Faxi wasn't dead, because Faxi said then, "You have done a great deed of bravery to have overcome me, Thorstein, because I have had ninety battles and have won all of them except for this one. I have won eighty times in duels that I have fought, but I am ninety years old now."

Thorstein didn't think it was any use to Thorstein for Faxi to babble any longer, if he could do anything about it. He ripped Faxi's innards out.

Now there is this to tell about Angantyr and Beli: they took a ship and rowed out into the sea and looked for Faxi and Thorstein, and found neither one for a long time. Then they came to where the sea was red, mingled with blood. They though that Faxi must have gone to the bottom and killed Thorstein there. And a moment later, they saw that something nasty was floating on the sea. They went to that spot and saw huge and hideous entrails floating there.

A little later Thorstein came up. By then he was so weary and overcome that he couldn't manage to float. They rowed towards him and pulled him up into the ship. He had little chance of surviving; he wasn't badly wounded, but his flesh was falling off his bones in clumps. They went back to the island and tried to help him. Soon he came to his senses. They went back to the island and searched for the slain, and there were no more than thirty men who could be healed.

Then they went to old man Brennir and thanked him for his assistance. Thorstein went to Brennir's smaller island to find the dwarf Sindri. He gave him good gifts, and they parted in the best of friendship. Thorstein took the dragon-ship Ellidi as his share of the booty, but Beli had the dragon-ship Ufi's Gift, and Angantyr took as much gold and silver as he liked for his own share. Thorstein gave Brennir, his kinsman, all the ships that they couldn't take with them, and they sailed away in three ships, home to Sogn, and stayed there for the winter.

CHAPTER XXIV

In spring they set out raiding. Angantyr asked where they should head for. He said that he thought that the eastern Baltic must be abandoned by vikings.

Beli said, "Then we shall sail west over the sea, because we have never raided there before."

Now they did so. As soon as they came to Orkney, they landed and raided, burned settlements, and plundered riches. They did great pillaging there, and everyone was afraid of them and ran away.

The jarl who had to govern the islands was named Herraud. When he heard of this plundering, he mustered his forces against them and traveled night and day, until they met on the island called Papa Westray[62]. At once a battle broke out between them. Neither side had the advantage. They fought for two days, so that no one could decide which of them would win.

It happened at last that the casualties began to grow on Herraud's side. Then his ships were cleared of men. The brothers boarded, and it happened at last that Jarl Herraud fell and almost all of his men.

Then they went through all the islands and assumed power over them. Afterwards, they prepared for the journey home. King Beli offered Thorstein the islands and offered to make him jarl over them, but he said that he didn't want that—"I would rather be a hersir and not be parted from you, than be named a jarl and live far away from you." Then Beli asked Angantyr to be jarl over the islands, and he accepted. He was made jarl over the islands and had to pay tribute each year.

Then they set course for home to Sogn and stayed there that winter. They maintained their own men well, both in weapons and in clothes. No men seemed more prominent than the sworn brothers. Children were born to them. The sons of Beli were named Helgi and Halfdan, and his daughter was Ingibjorg. She was the youngest of the children. Thorstein had a son named Fridthjof.

Harald grew up in the islands next to Grim, and as soon as he was of age, he began raiding and became the most famous man, although little is said of him in this saga. He held to his name and was called Harald Spear, and there are many men descended from him.

Thorstein, Beli, Grim, and Harald held their friendship as long as they lived.

CHAPTER XXV

Now there is this to tell about Jokul Njorfi's son: he ruled over Oppland when both Njorfi and Viking were dead. They had kept up their friendship well, until their dying days. Jokul acquired ships and money for himself and was the fiercest raider, and it went middlingly well with his forces, but no better. So it went for several years, that his name was the most renowned. He most often went on raids around the eastern Baltic.

Thorstein and Beli had not been home long before they prepared for a raid. They sailed south along the land that faces the Øresund, and raided in Germany through the summer. They did much pillaging and got much wealth there, in gold and silver and many other precious things. Then they intended to sail home, which they did. But when they had come to the entrance to the Limfjord, a storm came at them and swept them towards the open ocean, and the ships were quickly separated. The sea began to pour in on both sides, and all the men had to bale out the ship. It so happened that this storm tossed the dragon-ship Ellidi up on the island of Bornholm, alone.

At that time, Jokul came to that land with ten ships, all well equipped with weapons and crews. There's no need to ask what happened next:

Sagas of Fridthjof

Jokul had them attack Thorstein and his men. Thorstein was poorly prepared, because they were very weary from their trials and their sea voyage. The battle was both fierce and bloody. Jokul was the most eager and urged his men on and said that they would never have a better opportunity to attack Thorstein—"and if Thorstein gets away now, that will be forever thrown in our face." They attacked Thorstein and his men and didn't let up until all his men had fallen, so that there was no one left standing on the dragon-ship except for Thorstein alone. He still defended himself manfully.

For a long time, they didn't lay a wound on him. But it happened at last that they came so close to him that they attacked him with spear-thrusts. He knocked almost all of them away from himself, because the sword Angrvadil bit as it always did. Then Jokul made a fierce attack and stabbed his spear through his thigh. At that moment Thorstein struck at Jokul. That blow struck his arm in front of the elbow and cut his hand off. At that moment they were able to press Thorstein down with their shields and capture him.

By then, evening had come, so that they thought that it was not lawful to kill him.[63] Fetters were set on his feet, and his hands were tied with a bow-string. Twelve men were detailed to watch him through the night. When everyone had gone ashore except for these twelve men and Thorstein, he said, "Which would you prefer: to entertain me, or for me to entertain you?" They said that he wouldn't lack for entertainment, since he would die as soon as it was morning.[64]

Thorstein now thought about his situation, and it seemed to him that he was not in a good way. He said in a low voice, "How could I need you at any other time more than now, my comrade Sindri, if our friendship hadn't completely ended?"

Then darkness broke out over the guards, and next they were all asleep. Thorstein saw that Sindri was coming to the rear of the ship to him. He said, "You're in a bad way, Thorstein my comrade, and it's high time to save you." He blew on the lock and opened it. Then he cut the bowstring from him, and Thorstein was free. He took his sword, because he knew where he had put it away. Then he turned to the guards and killed them all.

At that, Sindri went away, and Thorstein took a boat for himself and rowed to land. He went away and came home to Sogn. Beli was glad to see him and thought that Thorstein had been pulled out of Hel.

Jokul awoke early in the morning and thought it would be good to take the prisoner and kill him. But when he got there, the prisoner was gone, and the guards were dead. It seemed to them that their "friend" had flown. Jokul sailed home and was not content with his journey; he lost Thorstein, and received a lasting disfigurement from which he never recovered. Since then he was called Jokul the One-Handed.

The sworn brothers, King Beli and Thorstein, summoned their forces and went to Oppland and sent word to Jokul, and staked out a field with hazel poles[65] for a battle with him. Jokul assembled his men, but many of Jokul's subjects stayed home, and they did that for the sake of friendship with Thorstein. When Jokul got few men, he did not trust himself to hold battle with them. He abandoned his lands and went to Normandy to William, his father-in-law. There he took the stewardship of a third of the kingdom. King Beli and Thorstein laid Oppland under their rule, and then went home and stayed there quietly.

Some time later, men whom Jokul had sent came from Normandy to meet Thorstein. They brought the message that Jokul asked for peace from Thorstein, and they should meet in the Limfjord with three ships each, and come to a settlement. That suited Thorstein's mind well, and he said that he was sorry to have had hostility with Jokul, for the sake of King Njorfi and his friendship with Viking.

The agreement was made. The messengers went home, and Thorstein prepared to set out in the summer. He had the dragon-ship Ellidi and two other ships. Beli felt that this journey wouldn't end well, since Jokul seemed treacherous and untrustworthy. His plan was to send spies to find out whether everything was true on Jokul's part, and he would follow them and meet them in the Øresund. So they did, and the spies came back and told them that Jokul's party was anchored in the Limfjord with three ships, and all was quiet with them. Then they went on their way to the fjord, and met up in the arranged place. They came to the agreement that all deaths, blows, and battles should cancel each other out, but that Jokul should take back his kingdom and should not pay tribute to any man. Thorstein's rule over Oppland should be returned to Jokul, as compensation for cutting off his hand. With these obligations they made peace. Jokul then went home to his kingdom and stayed there quietly.

Thorstein and Beli went home to Sogn and settled down in their own kingdom and gave up all their raiding. Ingibjorg, Thorstein's wife, had died, and Beli's daughter Ingibjorg bore her name. Fridthjof grew up with his father.

Thorstein had a daughter named Vefreyja.[66] She was fully grown when she came into the story, because she was begotten in the cave with Skellinefja, and she was raised there. She took after her mother in wisdom. She took Angrvadil after Thorstein her father.

Many famous men are descended from Thorstein. Everyone felt that Thorstein was the most celebrated man, and the bravest of those men who lived at that time.

With these words, we now end the story of Thorstein Vikingsson, and it is the most enjoyable saga.

THE SAGA OF FRIDTHJOF THE BOLD

CHAPTER I

So begins this saga: King Beli ruled the realm of Sogn. He had three children. One of his sons was named Helgi, and the other was Halfdan, but Ingibjorg was the name of his daughter. Ingibjorg was beautiful in appearance and wise in mind. She was the foremost of the king's children.

The shore extended some distance along the western side of the fjord, and there was a large estate there. That estate was called Balder's Meadow. There was a sanctuary and a great temple, with a high fence all around. Many idols were there, but Balder was the most honored. The heathen folk were so devout that no injury could be done there, neither to cattle nor to people. Men could not have any dealings with women there.

The king's estate was called Syrstrond. On the other side of the fjord stood an estate called Framnes. There lived the man named Thorstein, the son of Viking. His farm stood opposite from the king's seat. Thorstein and his wife had a son named Fridthjof. He was the tallest and strongest of all men, and skilled at games and sports from childhood. He was called Fridthjof the Bold. He was so well-liked that everyone wished him well.

The king's children were young when their mother died. Hilding was the name of a good farmer in Sogn. He offered to foster the king's daughter. She was raised there, well and carefully. She was called Ingibjorg the Fair. Fridthjof was also fostered with the farmer Hilding, and he and the king's daughter were foster-siblings. They surpassed other children.

King Beli began to let his wealth slip from his hands, because he was growing old. Thorstein held the stewardship of a third of the kingdom, and was the king's greatest source of strength and support. Thorstein held a feast for the king every third year, at great expense, and the king held a feast for Thorstein in the other two years.

Helgi, Beli's son, became a devout sacrificer early in life. The brothers weren't well-liked.

Thorstein had a ship that was named Ellidi. It held fifteen rowers on each side. The prow and stern were recurved like a bow, and the ship was as strong as an ocean-going vessel. The sides were spangled with iron. Fridthjof was so strong that he rowed with two oars in the bow of Ellidi, and every oar was thirteen ells long—but at the other benches, two men had to pull each oar. Fridthjof was thought to excel the other young men of that time. The king's sons were envious that he was more highly praised than they.

King Beli now became sick, and when his illness weighed down on him, he called on his sons and said to them, "This sickness will be the death of me. I want to ask this of you, that you keep the long-standing friends which I have had, because you seem to me to come up short in every way compared to the father and son, Thorstein and Fridthjof, both in wisdom and in bravery. You must raise a mound for my burial." After that Beli died.

After that, Thorstein became sick. He spoke to Fridthjof, his kinsman: "I will ask this of you, that you restrain your temper around the king's sons, as is befitting for the sake of their rank. But my heart tells me that this will turn out well. I want to have myself buried in a mound opposite King Beli's mound, on this side of the fjord, down by the sea. Then it will be quite easy for us to call out to each other when important events happen."

Fridthjof's sworn brothers[1] were named Bjorn and Asmund. They were big strong men.

A little later, Thorstein breathed his last. He was buried in a mound, as he had said before. Fridthjof inherited his land and wealth.

CHAPTER II

Fridthjof became the most celebrated man and proved himself valiantly in all trials. His sworn-brother Bjorn was the worthiest, and Asmund served them both. He inherited the ship Ellidi, his best possession, from his father, along with another possession, a gold ring. There was no ring more precious in Norway.

Fridthjof was such a magnificent man that most people reckoned that he was no less noble than the brothers, except for their kingly rank. For that reason, the brothers treated Fridthjof with coldness and hostility, and they found it troubling that he was called the better man, but they realized that Ingibjorg, their sister, and Fridthjof were falling in love.

It happened that the kings had to attend the feast at Fridthjof's estate at Framnes. And so it went, as usual, that he feasted everyone more richly than they merited. Ingibjorg was there, and she talked with Fridthjof for a long time. The king's daughter said to him, "You have a good gold ring."

"That's true," said Fridthjof.

After that the brothers went home, and their grudge against Fridthjof grew.

A little later, Fridthjof became very gloomy. His sworn brother Bjorn asked him what had happened. Fridthjof said that he had it in mind to ask for Ingibjorg: "although I have a lesser title than her brothers, yet I believe myself to be no less worthy than them."

Bjorn said, "Let's do this!"

Then Fridthjof went with some men to meet with the brothers. The kings were sitting on their father's mound.[2] Fridthjof greeted them well and stated his case right away, asking for the hand of their sister Ingibjorg. The kings answered: "It is not wise to pursue this request that we should give her to a man of no rank, and both of us absolutely refuse."

Fridthjof answered, "Then my errand is over quickly. But in turn it will happen that I will never again provide help to you, even if you need it."

They said that they would never care about that. Fridthjof went straight home and became cheerful again.

CHAPTER III

There was a king named Hring. He ruled over Ringerike; that was in Norway[3]. He was a powerful and honorable shire-king, although by then he was in his declining years. He said to his men, "I have heard

Saga of Fridthjof the Bold

that the sons of Beli have broken off their friendship with Fridthjof, who is more excellent than most men. Now I will send my men to meet with the kings and offer them a choice: they may submit to me and yield tribute, or else I will make war on them. It will be easy to conquer them, because neither of them is a match for me, neither in strength nor in cleverness. Yet it would be a great glory for me to destroy them in my old age."

After that, the messengers of King Hring went to meet the brothers and spoke thus: "King Hring sends you this message: you two shall send him tribute, or else he will invade your kingdom."

They said that they didn't want to learn in their youth what they didn't want to know in old age: how to serve him in disgrace. "Now we shall summon all the forces that we can get." And so it was done. But when it occurred to them that their forces were small, they sent Hilding[4], Fridthjof's foster-father, to Fridthjof. He was to ask him to join forces with the kings.

Fridthjof was sitting at *hnefataft*[5] when Hilding came. He said these words: "Our kings send you greetings, and they wish to have your assistance in the battle against King Hring, who wants to invade our kingdom, bringing tyranny and injustice."

Fridthjof didn't answer him and said to Bjorn, whom he was playing against, "There's a gap in your position, sworn brother! And you can't get out of it.[6] But instead, I will advance on the golden[7] piece and find out whether it is defended."

Hilding said, "King Helgi has ordered me to inform you, Fridthjof, that you must go on this war expedition, or you will suffer harsh consequences when they come back."

Bjorn then said, "There are two alternatives, sworn brother, and two ways to play."

Fridthjof said, "It would be advisable to attack the king-piece first. That won't be a doubtful choice."

Hilding got no other response to his message. He went back quickly to meet the kings and told them Fridthjof's answers. They asked Hilding what sense he could make out of these words. Hilding said, "When he spoke about the gap in the position, he must have been thinking about a gap in your forces. When he said that he would advance on the gold piece, that must mean Ingibjorg, your sister. Therefore guard her carefully. And when I promised him harsh consequences from you, Bjorn considered that to be one alternative, but Fridthjof said that the king-piece would be attacked first. He was talking about King Hring."

At once they set off. Before they left, they had Ingibjorg brought to Balder's Meadow, along with eight serving-women. They said that Fridthjof would not be so rash as to go to meet her there, "because no one is so foolhardy that he would do any damage to the sanctuary."

The brothers went south to Jaederen and encountered King Hring in Sokkensund[8]. What had made King Hring angriest was that the brothers had said that it seemed shameful to fight a man who was so old that he could not mount a horse without help.

CHAPTER IV

While the kings were away, Fridthjof dressed in his finery and put the good gold ring on his hand. Then the sworn brothers went down to the sea and launched Ellidi. Bjorn said, "Where shall we sail, sworn brother?"

Fridthjof said, "To Balder's Meadow, to amuse ourselves with Ingibjorg."

Bjorn said, "It isn't worth it for you to offend the god."

Fridthjof replied, "We'll risk it. I care for Ingibjorg's favor more than Balder's wrath."

After that, they rowed over the fjord and went up to Balder's Meadow and came into Ingibjorg's bower. She was sitting there with her eight maids. Fridthjof also had eight men. When they came there, everything was hung with rich fabric and costly tapestries. Ingibjorg stood up and said, "Fridthjof, how can you be so bold as to come here without my brothers' leave, and offend the gods?"

Fridthjof said, "That's as may be. But I care for your love more than the gods' wrath."

Ingibjorg answered, "You shall be welcome here, and all your men."

Then she gave him space to sit next to her, and drank to him with the finest wine, and so they all sat down and enjoyed themselves. Ingibjorg saw the good ring on his hand, and asked whether he owned the treasure. Fridthjof said that he did. She praised the ring greatly.

Fridthjof said, "I will give you the ring, if you will swear never to part with it, and to return it to me if you don't want to have it. And with it, we must each agree to be true to the other." With this plighting of troth, they exchanged rings.[9]

Fridthjof was often in Balder's Meadow overnight, and traveled between the estates every day, and enjoyed himself with Ingibjorg.[10]

CHAPTER V

Now it's time to tell about the brothers. They encountered King Hring, and he had greater forces. Men went between them and sought a settlement, so that no violence would break out. King Hring said that his will in the matter was that the kings should put themselves under his authority and give him Ingibjorg the Fair, their sister, along with a third of all that they owned. The kings agreed to this, for they saw that they were dealing with a powerful opponent. This settlement was bound by oaths. The wedding was to be in Sogn when King Hring would come to meet his betrothed. The brothers went home, along with their men, and were not at all happy with the outcome.

When Fridthjof believed that it was time for the brothers to come home, he said to the king's daughter, "You have given us a fine and fair welcome, and farmer Balder has not been bothered by us. But as soon as you find out that the kings have come home, spread out your fine cloths on the temple of the goddess[11], because it's the highest in the enclosure. We will see that from our estate."

The king's daughter said, "You have not followed the example of other men, but certainly we have to welcome our friends when you come."

Then Fridthjof went home. The next morning, he went outside early. When he came in, he spoke a verse:

> I must tell this
> to our trusty thanes:
> our pleasant cruises
> have been cut short.
> The stalwarts must not
> go sailing again,
> because the blankets
> bleach in the sun.

Then they went outside and saw that the entire roof of the temple of the goddess was covered with white linen cloths.

Bjorn said, "The kings must have come home now, and we won't be able to stay here in peace for much longer. I think it's a good idea to muster our forces." And so it was done. A crowd of people thronged there.

The brothers soon heard about the conduct of Fridthjof and his men. King Helgi said, "It seems incredible to me that Balder should suffer every shame from Fridthjof and his men. Now we shall send men to him and find out what settlement he will offer us. Otherwise we shall order him from our lands, for I don't see that our forces can fight his, for the time being."

Hilding, Fridthjof's foster-father, carried the kings' message to Fridthjof and his friends. Their message was: "As a settlement from you, Fridthjof, the kings wish to have you fetch home the tribute from Orkney, which has not been paid since Beli died. They need the money, as they are betrothing Ingibjorg, their sister, with a large dowry."

Fridthjof said, "The only thing keeping peace between us is respect for our elder kinsmen, but the brothers will show no faithfulness to us. I want to stipulate that all of our possessions be left in peace while I am away." And so it was promised and bound by oath.

Now Fridthjof prepared for his journey, and chose his men for their valor and the help they could provide. They were eighteen men all together. His men asked him whether he wouldn't prefer to go to King Helgi first and come to terms with him, and beg to turn away Balder's wrath. Fridthjof said, "I swear this oath: I will not beg for peace from King Helgi." After that he boarded Ellidi, and they set sail from Sognefjord.

But when Fridthjof had gone away, King Halfdan said to Helgi his brother, "Our rule would be stronger and better if Fridthjof were paid back for his crimes. We two will burn his farm, and send a storm at him and his men, so that they will never be saved."

Helgi said that this should be done. At once they burned up all the estate at Framnes, and plundered all its wealth. Then they sent for two witches[12], Heid and Hamglama[13], and gave them money to send such fierce weather at Fridthjof and his men that they should all be lost at sea. The women worked their magic and pulled themselves up onto a platform, chanting and working spells.

CHAPTER VI

When Fridthjof and his men sailed out of the Sognefjord, sharp winds and a great storm blew up. Then the waves rose up very high. The ship went very fast, because it slid swiftly over the water and was the best ship on the ocean. Then Fridthjof spoke a verse:

> From Sognefjord I let slip
> the swarthy wave-horse—
> the maids enjoyed their mead
> amidst Balder's bower.
> Now the storm-winds sharpen;
> though Ellidi sinks and founders,
> may the brides who bear us love
> have a beautiful day!

Bjorn said, "It would be nice if you could do something other than sing about the maidens of Balder's Meadow."

"That won't calm this storm," said Fridthjof.

The storm drove them north to the sounds near those islands called the Solunds. The wind was then at its harshest. Then Fridthjof said:

> The sea starts to swell,
> striking up to the clouds,
> old magics make waves
> move from their home.
> In so wild a windstorm
> I will not challenge Ægir[14];
> let the surf-wrapped Solunds
> shelter our crewmen.

They anchored in the lee of the Solunds and intended to wait there, and the wind dropped immediately. Then they turned the ship around and set out from the lee of the islands. They felt hopeful about their journey, for they had a suitably favorable wind for a while. But it happened that the wind grew brisker. Then Fridthjof said,

> In former days
> in Framnes,
> I manned the oars
> to meet Ingibjorg.
> Now I shall sail
> in the stiff breeze,
> let the light sea-beast°   *sea-beast*: ship
> leap beneath me.

And when they had come a long way out onto the ocean, then the sea became incredibly violent a second time, and a huge squall blew up, with such great snowstorms that one end of the ship couldn't be seen from the other end. Water poured into the ship, so that the men were constantly baling out the ship. Then Fridthjof said:

> Swells can't be seen—
> we sailed out on the foam,
> well-known war-companions—
> because of weather-magic.
> Now sailors set to bailing,
> the Solunds far behind us:
> eighteen men in all,
> Ellidi's defenders.

Bjorn said, "He who travels widely meets with all sorts of fates." "That's the truth, sworn brother!" said Fridthjof, and he spoke:

> Helgi makes the heaving
> hoar-maned waves surge—
> it's not like embracing brides
> in Balder's Meadow.
> They love me in unlike ways,
> that lord, and Ingibjorg:

to offer her what's fitting
shall be good fortune for me.

"It may be," said Bjorn, "that she thinks of something higher for you. But this isn't bad to know now."

Fridthjof said that it would be a chance to test good sailors, although it would be more enjoyable to be in Balder's Meadow. They prepared themselves manfully, for they were mighty men assembled together, and the ship was the best that has ever been in the Northlands. Fridthjof spoke a verse:

> Swells can't be seen
> as we sail westwards.
> All the ocean seems to me
> like embers smoldering.
> Sea-billows are streaming,
> swan's land° throws up mounds.   *swan's land:* sea
> Now Ellidi tosses
> on towering breakers.

Then the seas came breaking over the ship, so that they all had to bale. Fridthjof spoke a verse:

> If in the swan's slopes°   *swan's slopes:* sea
> I must sink deep,
> the maid will mourn me
> and drink much to me—
> bilge-water surges
> are swamping Ellidi—
> there, where the linens
> lay in the sun.

Bjorn said, "Do you think that the maidens of Sogn will shed many tears for you?"

Fridthjof said, "It certainly crossed my mind."

Just then a surge struck them, so that torrents fell into the ship, but it helped that the ship was so good, and the sailors were hardy men between the gunwales. Then Bjorn spoke a verse:

> It's not as if some dame
> wants to drink to your fame,
> or bids you be bolder,
> that bright rings' holder.°   *ring's holder*: woman
> Salty are the eyes
> when briny seas rise.
> Strong arms give way,
> eyes sting from spray.[15]

Asmund said, "Even if your arms are tired, we don't care. You didn't pity us when we rubbed our eyes, when you two got up so early for your trips to Balder's Meadow."

"So why don't you speak a verse, Asmund?" said Fridthjof.

"I can't do that," said Asmund, but he spoke a verse:

> There were sharp tugs on the sail
> as the sea battered this boat.
> I must labor in this longship
> alone, with eight others.
> It was better, bringing breakfast
> to the bowers of the ladies,
> than baling out Ellidi
> as the breakers surge.

"You're hardly underrating your own efforts," said Fridthjof, laughing. "But you just now showed that you're descended from thralls, since you'd rather do the cooking."

Then the wind blew up anew, so that the crewmen thought that the whitecaps crashing against the ship from all sides looked more like huge mountain peaks than waves. Fridthjof spoke:

> I sat on a bolster
> in Balder's Meadow,
> sang what I could

> for the king's daughter.
> Now I will rest on
> Ran's trusty bed,
> while another lies
> by lady Ingibjorg.

Bjorn said, "Now these are strong words, sworn brother! There is fear in your words now, and that's a bad thing for such a good companion."

Fridthjof said, "It's neither fear nor anxiety, although it may be said about our pleasure trips—and it may be true—that they were made more often than necessary. But most men in our position would think that death was more likely than survival. All the same, I'll answer you with something." And he spoke a verse:

> I paid the price for these trips,
> when proud Ingibjorg came
> to meet me—but not you—
> with eight maids-in-waiting.
> We placed pure gold rings together,
> pledged troth in Balder's Meadow;
> the keeper of Halfdan's kingdom°   *keeper of Halfdan's kingdom:* Balder
> was close at hand that day.

Bjorn said, "We must be content with what's been done, sworn brother."

Then such a great wave came breaking over the ship that it tore loose the gunwale and both the prow and the stern, and it washed four men overboard, and all were lost. Then Fridthjof said:

> Bow and stern are broken,
> battered by great waves,
> four swains sank down
> into the seas' depths.

"Now it appears likely," said Fridthjof, "that some of our men will journey to Ran[16]. We will not appear properly attired when we come there, unless we prepare ourselves bravely. I think it's advisable for every man to have some gold on him." Then he broke apart the ring, Ingibjorg's Gift, and divided it with his men and spoke a verse:

> And so the red-gold ring
> of the rich father of Halfdan
> must be broken, before
> Ægir blots us out.
> He'll see gold on his guests,
> if good lodging we need,
> which helps splendid heroes
> in the halls of Ran.

Bjorn said, "Such things aren't so certain, but it's not unlikely."

Fridthjof and his men found that the ship was gliding quickly, but they didn't know where they had come to, because such darkness lay around them on all sides that one couldn't see the prow from the stern, with foaming seas and fierce gales, frost and snowstorms and immense cold. Then Fridthjof climbed up the mast and said to his fellows when he came back down, "I saw a most wondrous sight. A huge whale is swimming in a ring around the ship. I suspect that we must be approaching some land or other, and it wants to block us from landing. I think that King Helgi has not dealt with us in a friendly way, and he must have sent us no friendly message. I see two women on the back of the whale, and they must have caused this violent storm with their wickedest spells and chants. Now we must test which is greater, our luck or their sorcery. You must steer as straight as possible, and I shall thrash these evil spirits with a cudgel." And he spoke a verse:

> I see two troll-women
> on the tossing waves;
> Helgi has had them
> sent hither to us.
> Ellidi's keel shall
> cleave them asunder,
> rip them into pieces,
> before reaching land.

It is said that the ship Ellidi had been magically charmed, so that she had learned to understand human speech. Bjorn said, "Now men may see how honorably the brothers have treated us."

And then Bjorn took the rudder, but Fridthjof seized a pole and leaped into the prow and spoke a verse:

> Hail, Ellidi!
> Hurdle the waves!
> Break the troll-women's
> teeth and foreheads,
> the cheeks and chops
> of these churlish hags,
> one or both of
> these ogresses' legs!

At once he struck at one of the shape-shifters with the pole, and the prow of Ellidi struck the back of the other, and both of their backs were broken. The whale dived into the ocean and swam away, and he didn't see it again.

Then the weather began to calm, but the ship was waterlogged. Fridthjof called to his men and ordered them to bail out the ship. Bjorn said that it was no use taking the trouble to do that.

"Guard against fear now, sworn brother!" said Fridthjof, "It has long been the warrior's way to lend a hand while he can, whatever happens." Fridthjof spoke a verse:

> You've no need, warriors,
> to worry about death.
> Be most happy,
> my heroes all!
> I've seen in my dreams
> and surely know
> that I will marry
> Ingibjorg.

Then they baled out the ship. They had come near to land. Rain and snow were still coming against them. Fridthjof took the two oars in the bow and rowed them most mightily. The weather brightened, and they saw that they had arrived in Eynhallow Sound[17], and they landed there. The sailors were quite exhausted, and Fridthjof was so mighty that he carried eight men out of reach of the tides. Bjorn carried two men, and Asmund carried one. Then Fridthjof said,

> I hauled eight
> exhausted warriors
> to the hearth-fire
> in howling winds.
> Now I've spread the sail
> out on the sand.
> It's not easy to struggle
> against the sea's might.

CHAPTER VII

Angantyr was at Evie[18] when Fridthjof and his men came to land. This was their custom: when Angantyr drank, a man had to sit outside his drinking-hall, across from the smoke-hole, and turn to face into the wind and keep watch. He had to drink from an animal's horn, and another horn was filled when the first one was drained. The man who held the watch when Fridthjof landed was named Hallvard. Hallvard saw the coming of Fridthjof and his men and spoke a verse:

> I see men
> in the mighty storm:
> six bale Ellidi
> and seven row.
> One like Fridthjof,
> fearless in war,
> is perched in the prow
> and pulls at the oars.

And when he had drained the horn, he threw it into the hall through the window, and said to the woman who served drink:

Saga of Fridthjof the Bold

> Pick up off the floor
> this overturned horn!
> I've drunk it all down,
> delicate lady.
> I see storm-worn
> sailing men—
> I must help them
> to make harbor.

The jarl heard what Hallvard said, and he asked for news. Hallvard answered, "Men have landed here, and they are very exhausted, but I think they are good warriors. And one is so strong that he carried the others to land."

The jarl said, "Go to meet them and greet them fittingly, if that is Fridthjof, son of my friend the hersir Thorstein, who is renowned in all accomplishments."

Then the man named Atli, a great viking, began to speak: "Now we shall test what they say, that Fridthjof has sworn an oath that he must not be the first to beg for peace." There were ten men together, bad men and fierce. They often went berserk.

When the two sides met, they picked up their weapons. Then Atli said, "Fridthjof! Now it's time to make your stand against us, for 'eagles claw each other when face to face'[19], Fridthjof! And now it's best to keep your word, and not ask for peace." Fridthjof turned to face them and spoke a verse:

> You can't keep us
> cowering here,
> you fear-filled,
> freakish islanders.[20]
> I'd rather dare
> ten dreadful foes,
> standing alone,
> than sue for peace.

Then Hallvard came up and said, "The jarl wishes for you all to be made welcome, and no one shall challenge you."

Fridthjof said that they would welcome that, but that he was ready for either peace or war.

After that they went to meet the jarl, and he welcomed Fridthjof and all his men. They stayed with him through the winter and were well honored. He often asked about their voyage. Bjorn spoke a verse:

> As the cold sea-spray
> crashed over us,
> we blithe heroes
> baled on both sides
> for eighteen days.

The jarl said, "You have had a narrow escape from King Helgi. Evil may be expected from such kings, who can do nothing else than destroy men with sorcery. And I know that that is your errand here, Fridthjof: you have been sent to collect tribute. I will quickly give you the answer that King Helgi shall get no tribute from me. But you shall have as much wealth from me as you want, and you may call that tribute if you want, or call it something else if you prefer."

Fridthjof said that he would accept the money.

CHAPTER VIII

Now it shall be told what happened in Norway while Fridthjof was away. The brothers had the farm at Framnes completely burned. But as the sisters were working their spells, they tumbled down from the platform, and both of them had broken backs.

That autumn, King Hring came north to Sogn for his wedding. That was a noble feast, when he wedded Ingibjorg.[21] He asked Ingibjorg, "Where did that good ring come from, which you have on your hand?"

She said that her father had owned it.

The king said, "That is Fridthjof's Gift. Take it off your hand at once, for you won't be lacking gold when you come to Alfheim."

She gave the ring to Helgi's wife, and begged her to give it to Fridthjof when he should come back. King Hring went home afterwards with his bride, and loved her very much.

CHAPTER IX

In the spring, Fridthjof left the Orkneys, and he and Angantyr parted in friendship. Hallvard went with Fridthjof. When they came to Norway, Fridthjof heard that his farm had been burned, and when he came to Framnes, he spoke: "My home here has been charred, and it's no friends of mine who have turned it this color." And he spoke a verse:

> Daring companions
> all drank together
> with my father
> at Framnes, once.
> Now I see the farm
> by flames burned.
> I must pay back
> the princes' evil.

Then he asked his men to decide what to do now, but they asked him to lead. He said that first they would pay the tribute. At once they rowed over the fjord to Syrstrond. There they heard that the kings were at Balder's Meadow, sacrificing to the goddesses[22]. Bjorn and Fridthjof went up there, and they asked Hallvard and Asmund in the meantime to break up all the ships in the area, small and large, and they did so.

Then Fridthjof and Bjorn went to the doors of the temple in Balder's Meadow. Fridthjof wanted to go in. Bjorn asked him to be careful, if he meant to go in alone. Fridthjof asked him to stay outside and stand guard in the meantime, and spoke a verse:

> I will go alone
> into the farm
> to find the king—
> I crave no help.
> Fling fire into
> this fighter's house,
> if I've not returned
> before twilight.

Bjorn answered, "Well spoken."

Then Fridthjof went inside and saw that few people were in the goddesses' hall. The kings were at the sacrifice to the goddesses, and sat there drinking. There was a fire on the floor, and their wives sat by the fire and warmed the idols, and some they anointed and wiped with towels.

Fridthjof went before King Helgi and said, "You'll want to have your tribute now." He brought up the purse that the silver was in and slammed it into his nose, so that two teeth were knocked out of Helgi's mouth, and he fell out of the high seat, unconscious. Halfdan grabbed him so that he didn't fall into the fire. Then Fridthjof spoke a verse:

> Accept this tribute,
> o stately lord!
> Take it in your teeth,
> don't trouble us further.
> The silver is in
> this sack's bottom,
> as Bjorn and I have
> both resolved.

Few people were in the room, for most of them were drinking in another place. But as Fridthjof was leaving the hall, he saw the good ring on the hand of Helgi's wife, as she was warming Balder at the fire. Fridthjof grabbed at the ring, but it was stuck fast on her hand, and he dragged her along the floor toward the doors, but Balder fell into the fire. Halfdan's wife quickly clutched at Helgi's wife, and then the idol that she had been warming fell into the fire. Now both idols caught fire because they had been anointed, and the flames shot up to the roof so that the house caught fire. Fridthjof got the ring before he went out.

Bjorn asked what had happened when he went in. Fridthjof held up the ring and spoke a verse:

> Helgi was battered by a blow,
> the bag struck the rascal's nose.
> Halfdan's sib fell swooning,
> sinking from the high-seat.

> Balder was left burning,
> but I brought the ring out first.
> Then I heaved a hooked branch
> out of the hearth-fire's embers.

People say that Fridthjof had thrust a burning board onto the bark on the roof, so that all the hall caught fire, and he spoke a verse:

> Let's set out for the shoreline,
> let strong plans be laid;
> black flames are billowing
> in the midst of Balder's Meadow.

After that they went to sea.

CHAPTER X

As soon as King Helgi came to his senses, he ordered his men to pursue Fridthjof and kill all his companions: "That man has forfeited his life, for he has spared no sanctuary." The kings' guard was summoned with a trumpet call, and when they arrived at the hall, they saw that it was burning. Halfdan went to the hall with some of his men, and King Helgi went after Fridthjof and his men. They got to the ships and had them shoved out to sea. King Helgi and his men found that all their ships were damaged, and they had to head back to land, and some men were lost.

King Helgi became so angry that he was possessed by rage. He bent his bow and nocked an arrow and meant to shoot at Fridthjof, but he bent the bow with such great strength that both tips broke off. As soon as Fridthjof saw that, he picked up two of Ellidi's oars and thrust them down in the sea so hard that both broke, and he spoke a verse:

> I kissed the young
> Ingibjorg,
> Beli's daughter,
> in Balder's Meadow.

> Now the oars
> on Ellidi
> shall both burst
> like the bow of Helgi.

After that a wind sprang up, blowing down the fjord. They hoisted the sail and sailed, and Fridthjof said to them that they should prepare themselves, as best they could, to not be able to live there any longer. Then they sailed out of the Sognefjord. Fridthjof spoke a verse:

> We sailed from Sognefjord
> just a short time ago.
> Then the flames were flickering
> in our father's inheritance,
> but fires begin to blaze now
> in the midst of Balder's hall.
> Now I've been named an outlaw;
> I know I must be, truly.

Bjorn said to Fridthjof, "What shall we do for a living now, sworn brother?"

"I cannot stay here in Norway. I want to learn the warrior's way and turn viking."

They explored islands and skerries through the summer, and so gained riches and fame for themselves. In the autumn they sailed to Orkney, and Angantyr welcomed them, and they stayed there through the winter.

When Fridthjof had left Norway, the kings held an assembly and declared Fridthjof an outlaw throughout all their realms, and they took all his property for themselves. King Halfdan stayed at Framnes and rebuilt the estate that he had burned. They also restored all of Balder's Meadow, but it was a long time before the fire was extinguished. What pained King Helgi the worst was that the idols were burned up. It required great expense before Balder's Meadow was completely rebuilt as it was before. King Helgi now resided at Syrstrond.

CHAPTER XI

Fridthjof earned riches and renown wherever he went. He killed wicked men and savage vikings, but let farmers and merchants live in peace.[23] Once again he was called Fridthjof the Bold. He gained a large and very capable force, and became very wealthy.

But when Fridthjof had been raiding for four years, he sailed out of the east and anchored in the Oslofjord. Fridthjof said that he would go on land, "but you should set out raiding this winter, for raiding is becoming tiresome to me. I will go to Oppland and find King Hring and speak with him. But you must come visit me in the summer, and I will come back here on the first day of summer."

Bjorn said, "This plan is not wise, yet you must decide. I want us to go north to Sognefjord and kill both those kings, Helgi and Halfdan."

Fridthjof answered, "That would come to nothing. I would rather go to meet King Hring and Ingibjorg."

Bjorn said, "I am unwilling to risk having you go into his power alone, for Hring is wise and high-born, though rather elderly."

Fridthjof said that he would decide, "and you shall lead our forces in the meantime, Bjorn." They did as he asked.

Fridthjof went to Oppland in the autumn, for he was curious to see the love between King Hring and Ingibjorg. Before he came there, he put on a great shaggy cloak over his clothes. He had two staffs in his hands and a hood over his face, and he made himself look very old. As soon as he met some shepherds, he went up shyly and asked, "Where are you from?"

They replied, "We have a home in Streituland, at the king's seat."

The old man asked, "Is he a mighty king, this Hring?"

They answered, "You seem old enough to us that you ought to know what sort of man King Hring is in every way."

The old man said that he had paid more attention to salt-burning[24] than to royalty. Then he went to the hall, and at the end of the day, he went into the hall. He appeared to be decrepit. He took a place at the edge of the crowd, let the hood fall over his face, and waited.[25]

King Hring said to Ingibjorg, "A man has come into the hall, much taller than other men."

The queen answered, "That is no great news here."

The king spoke with the servant who stood before the table: "Go and ask who this cloaked man is, and where he comes from, and where his kinfolk live."

The lad dashed across the floor to the man who had come and asked, "What is your name, man? Where were you last night, and who are your kin?"

The cloaked man answered, "You ask many questions, boy! Can you use any discernment if I tell you the answers?"

He replied that he could do it well.

The cloaked man said, "I am called Thief. I was with Wolf last night, and I was raised in Straits."[26]

The boy dashed back to the king and told him the cloaked man's answers. The king said, "You perceive well, boy! I know the district called Straits, and being in Straits may not ease the mind of most men. This must be a wise man, and he seems most worthy to me."

The queen said that it was unbelievable of him—"that you desire so eagerly to talk with every old man that comes here. What worth can he have?"

The king said, "You don't know any better than I do. I can tell that he thinks more than he talks, and keeps a sharp eye out all around him."

After that the king sent a man for him, and the cloaked man went into the hall before the king, rather bent, and greeted him in a low voice. The king said, "What is your name, tall man?"

The cloaked man spoke a verse:

> I was called Peace-Thief
> when I prowled with vikings,
> but War-Thief
> when I made widows mourn,
> Spear-Thief when I
> showered javelins,
> Battle-Thief when I
> banded with warriors,
> Skerry-Thief when I
> sacked far islands,
> Hel-Thief when I
> harmed small children,

Fallen-Thief when I
frightened men.
Since then I have strayed
with old salt-burners,
needing help,
before here I came.

The king said, "From many things have you taken the name of a thief. Where were you in the night, and where is your home?"

The cloaked man answered, "I was raised in Straits. My heart encouraged me to come here, but I am homeless."

The king answered, "Maybe you have been in Straits for some time, but it also might be that you have been raised in Frith.[27] You must have been in the forest at night, for there is no farmer in this region named Wolf. But since you say that you have no home, it may be that your home seems unworthy to you, since you have come here."

Then Ingibjorg said, "Go elsewhere for lodging, Thief! Or go to the guest-house."

The king said, "I am old enough that I can decide who is a guest here. Take off your hood, new arrival! And sit on my other side."

The queen replied, "Now you've become senile, since you've arranged for a beggar to sit next to you."

Thief said, "That isn't fitting, lord! As the queen says, I am more accustomed to salt-makers than sitting next to chieftains."

The king said, "Do as I bid, for I will decide this time."

Thief let the cloak fall from him. Underneath, he had on a dark blue tunic, and he had the good ring on his hand. He had a wide silver belt around his waist, and on it was a great purse with bright silver coins. He was girded with a sword at his side, and wore a great leather cap on his head. He had downcast eyes, and hair all over his face.

"Now I call that a better way to go about," said the king. "Queen, you must give him a good mantle, fitting to him."

The queen said, "That is your decision, lord! But I don't think much of this thief."

Then he was given a good mantle to cover himself, and he sat in the high seat next to the king. The queen blushed red as blood when she saw the good ring, although she didn't want to exchange any words with

Sagas of Fridthjof

him. But the king was quite cheerful with him and said, "You have a good ring on your hand, and you must have been boiling salt for a long time to get it."

He said, "That is all the inheritance I have from my father."

"It may be," said the king, "that you have more than that. I suppose that few salt-burners are equal to you, unless old age has sapped my eyesight considerably."

Thief was there through the winter and was treated with great honor, and all men liked him well. He was generous with money and cheerful with all men. The queen spoke little with him, but the king was always pleased with him.

It happened once that King Hring and his queen had to go to a feast, along with many of his men. The king said to Thief, "Would you rather come with us or stay at home?"

He said that he would rather go with them.

"I prefer that," said the king.

They set out on their journey, and they had to travel over a frozen lake. Thief said to the king, "The ice looks treacherous to me, and I think crossing it would be ill-advised."

The king said, "It's often that you are thinking of us."

A moment later, all the ice broke underneath them. Thief rushed to them and pulled the wagon and everything that was on it and in it towards himself. Both the king and the queen were sitting there. All of this Thief pulled up onto the ice, and along with it the horses that were hitched to it. King Hring said, "That was a brave deed to pull us out of the water, Thief! Not Fridthjof the Bold could have taken hold more strongly, had he been here. Men like you are the boldest of retainers."

Now they came to the feast, and everything there went uneventfully, and the king went home with worthy gifts.

Midwinter passed, and when spring came, the weather began warming. The forests began flowering, and grasses began growing, and ships could sail among lands.[28]

CHAPTER XII

One day, the king said to his guard, "I want you to come out into the forest with me today, to enjoy ourselves by viewing this fair landscape."

Saga of Fridthjof the Bold

And so they did. The king and a multitude of men scattered out through the forest. As it turned out, the king and Fridthjof were both together by themselves in the forest, far from other men. The king said he was feeling sleepy, "and I will sleep."

Thief answered, "Let's go home, lord! That is more suitable to a man's dignity than lying outside."

The king said, "I can't allow that." Then he lay down and fell fast asleep and snored loudly.

Thief sat next to him and drew his sword from its scabbard, and flung it far away from him. A while later, the king sat up and said, "Wasn't it so, Fridthjof, that many things came into your mind? But you solved the problem rightly. You shall now have high rank among us here. I recognized you from the first evening that you came into our hall. And you must not part from us quickly. Something great lies in store for you."[29]

Fridthjof said, "My lord, you have treated me well and friendly, but I must go away soon, for my forces are coming shortly to meet me, as I had previously arranged."

Then they rode home from the forest. The king's guardsmen gathered around them. They went home to the hall and drank well. It was revealed to all the people that Fridthjof the Bold had been there through the winter.

Early one morning, there was a knocking at the door of the hall where the king slept and the queen and many other people. The king asked who was calling at the doors. The man who was outside said, "It's Fridthjof, and now I am ready to be on my way." The door was opened, and Fridthjof came in and spoke a verse:

> Now I must give you great thanks.
> You granted a splendid—
> this roamer is ready to leave—
> refuge to this feeder of eagles.°
> I will remember Ingibjorg
> always, while we two live—
> fare well!—but we are fated
> to furnish treasures, not kisses.

feeder of eagles: warrior

Then he tossed the good ring to Ingibjorg and told her to keep it.

The king smiled at these verses and said, "And it's true that you thanked her for your winter lodging, better than you thanked me—yet she has not been more friendly to you than I." Then the king sent his servants to fetch food and drink, and said that they should eat and drink before Fridthjof went away. "Sit up, my queen! Be cheerful."

She said that she didn't feel like having a meal so early.

The king said, "We must now all dine together." And so they did.

And when they had drunk for a while, King Hring said, "I want you to stay here, Fridthjof! For my sons are still children, and I am old and not fit to guard the land if anyone attacks this kingdom in force."

Fridthjof said, "I must go soon, lord!" And he spoke a verse:

> King Hring, live
> hale and long,
> highest noble
> under heaven's cloak.
> Keep well, ruler,
> your wife and lands,
> I shall never see
> Ingibjorg again.

Then King Hring said:

> Don't depart from here,
> dearest of nobles,
> don't flee, Fridthjof,
> with fretful heart.
> I will furnish you
> with fine treasures,
> surely more splendid
> than you sought to have.

And then he said:

> To good Fridthjof,
> I give my wife,

and with her, all
my wealth and goods.

Fridthjof interrupted him and said in reply:

These treasures
I will not take,
unless, dear ruler,
you were deathly ill.

The king said, "I would not give them to you unless I knew that it was so—I am ill. I make this arrangement for you to enjoy best, for you are above all men in Norway. I will also grant you the title of king, for her brothers will bestow worse honors upon you, and be less willing to give you the woman's hand than I."

Fridthjof said, "Have great thanks for your good deed, lord, greater than I hoped for! But I want no more than the name and title of jarl."

Then King Hring joined hands with Fridthjof and gave him rulership over the kingdom that he had ruled, and with that the title of jarl. Fridthjof was to rule there until the sons of King Hring had come of age to rule their kingdom.

King Hring lay sick for a short while, and when he died, there was much grieving for him in the kingdom. Then a howe was raised for him and much wealth was laid inside, as he had requested. Fridthjof held a great feast, to which his men came, and King Hring's funeral feast and Ingibjorg's and Fridthjof's wedding feast were held together. After that, Fridthjof took up the rule of the kingdom, and he was a greatly renowned man there. He and Ingibjorg had many children.

The kings of Sogn, Ingibjorg's brothers, heard the news that Fridthjof held the throne of Ringerike and had married Ingibjorg their sister. Helgi said to Halfdan, his brother, that it was a great abomination and affront that the son of a hersir[30] should marry her. They summoned great forces and went to Ringerike with them, and intended to kill Fridthjof and claim all the kingdom.

But when Fridthjof became aware of this, he summoned his forces and said to the queen, "New unrest has come into our kingdom. However it may end, I do not wish to see resentment in you."

She answered, "It has come to this: I hold you highest."[31]

Bjorn came from the east to Fridthjof's aid, and they went into battle. It happened, as before, that Fridthjof was foremost in perilous situations. He and King Helgi traded blows, and Fridthjof killed him. Then Fridthjof had peace-shields[32] held up, and the battle stopped.

Fridthjof said to King Halfdan, "There are two great choices before you: either you surrender everything into my power, or else you get death like your brother. It seems that I have a better case than either of you." Halfdan chose to place himself and his kingdom under Fridthjof's rule.

Now Fridthjof took power in the kingdom of Sogn, and Halfdan had to be a hersir in Sogn and yield tribute to Fridthjof, while Fridthjof governed Ringerike. Fridthjof was given the title of king over Sogn when he turned Ringerike over to the sons of King Hring. After that, he gained Hordaland for his own. He and his wife had two sons, Gunnthjof and Hunthjof. They became great men in their own right.

And now, here ends the saga of Fridthjof the Bold.

THE TALE OF VIKAR
(chapters 3, 4, 5, and 7 of *Gautreks saga*)

CHAPTER III

Hunthjof was the name of a king who ruled over Hordaland. He was the son of Fridthjof the Bold and Ingibjorg the Fair. He had three sons. Herthjof was the name of one of his sons, who later was king of Hordaland. Another was named Geirthjof, king of Oppland, and the third was Fridthjof, king of Telemark. These were all mighty kings and great warriors, but King Herthjof was above them in intelligence and forethought. He was away on raids for a long time, and from this he became highly renowned.

At that time, there was a king in Agder named Harald, a mighty king. He was called Harald the Agder-King. His son was named Vikar; he was young and promising then.

There was a man named Storvirk; he was the son of Starkad Ala-Warrior. Starkad was a cunning giant. He kidnapped Alfhild, the daughter of King Alf, from Alfheim. King Alf then called on Thor, so that Alfhild might come back.[1] Thor killed Starkad and returned Alfhild home to her father, but she was with child. She raised her son, who was named Storvirk, as was mentioned earlier. He was a handsome man, although dark-haired, and bigger and stronger than other men. He was a great raider. He came to the household of Harald, the king of Agder, and took charge of his lands' defenses. King Harald gave him the island called Thruma[2], in Agder, and there Storvirk lived. He was away on raids for a long time, but at times he was with king Harald.

Storvirk kidnapped Unni, the daughter of jarl Freki of Halogaland. Then he went home to his estate in Thruma. They had a son, who was named Starkad. The sons of Jarl Freki, Fjori and Fyri, went against Storvirk and secretly came to his estate at night with a host. They burned the estate with Storvirk inside, along with Unni their sister and all the

Tale of King Vikar

men there, because they didn't dare open the door and were afraid that Storvirk would escape. They sailed away by night and went northwards along the coast. On the second day after they departed, a storm blew up at them, and they wrecked on the submerged rocks off Stad, and all their crews were lost.

Starkad, the son of Storvirk, was young when his father perished, and King Harald took him into fosterage with his household. So said Starkad about that:

> I was a boy, when
> they burned indoors
> full many seafarers,
> my father among them;
> beside the shore
> he sleeps on Thruma,
> the hardy hero
> of Harald Agder-King.

> His brothers in law burned
> the breaker of rings°:
> Fjori and Fyri,
> Freki's heirs,
> the brothers of Unni,
> my own mother.

breaker of rings: generous lord

CHAPTER IV

Herthjof the king of Hordaland and his forces moved secretly against King Harald at night and killed him treacherously, but they took his son Vikar as a hostage. King Herthjof placed all the realm that King Harald had had under his own rule, and he forcibly took the sons of many powerful men as hostages, and took tribute from all the kingdom.

Grani was the name of a mighty man in King Herthjof's forces. He was called Horsehair-Grani. He lived on the island in Hordaland which was called Fenhring, at the farm which was called Ask. He captured Starkad Storvirksson, and brought him to Fenhring. Starkad was three years old then, and he stayed on Fenhring with Horsehair-Grani for nine years. So says Starkad:

> When Herthjof
> with Harald had dealt,
> betrayed his trust
> through treachery,
> Agder's prince
> he deprived of his soul;
> he bound his sons
> in bonds and fetters.
>
> I was taken away,
> three winters old,
> to Hordaland
> by Horsehair-Grani;
> at Ask I began
> to grow up,
> I knew no kinsman
> for nine winters.

King Herthjof was a great warrior and was away raiding for a long time, and there was a great risk that his kingdom would be invaded. He had beacons built on the mountains and set men to tend them and set the beacons alight, if hostilities were to break out. Vikar tended the beacon on Fenhring with three men. They had to light the first beacon, if an invading host was seen, and then each would be lit from the other.

When Vikar had tended the beacon for a short while, he went one morning to Ask and met Starkad Storvirksson, his foster-brother. He was remarkably large. He was a laggard and a coal-biter[3] and lay on the floor by the fire. At the time he was twelve years old. Vikar picked him up off the floor and gave him weapons and clothes and measured his size, because he thought that he had grown amazingly large since he had come to Ask. Starkad and Vikar then got a ship for themselves and sailed away at once. So said Starkad:

Tale of King Vikar

I gained strength
in my growing arms,
got long legs
and a loathsome head,
as I sat daydreaming
down on the floor,
an idle one,
unaware of much.

Until Vikar came
from tending the beacon,
Herthjof's hostage,
the hall he entered;
at our meeting
he commanded me
to stand up straight
and speak to him.

He measured my size
with the span of his hands,
reckoned my arms' reach
to the wrist-joints.
My hair had grown,
hanging from my chin.

Here Starkad tells of how he had a beard when he was twelve.

Then Starkad got up, and Vikar gave him weapons and clothes, and they went to the ship. After that Vikar summoned men to help him, and they were twelve men all together. They were all champion warriors, and skilled at single combat. So said Starkad:

Then Harald's heirs
on Hildigrim called,
sent a summons
to Sorkvir and Grettir,
Erp and Ulf,
An and Skuma,

> Hroi and Hrotti
> Herbrand's sons,
>
> Styr and Steinthor
> from Stad in the north;
> old Gunnolf Blaze
> was also there.
> Thirteen warriors
> we were in all;
> you've seldom seen
> more splendid men.

Then King Vikar went with his forces to meet King Herthjof. When the king heard about this threat, then he had his own men prepare themselves. King Herthjof had a great farmhouse, and it was well fortified, so that it was almost a castle or fort. There were more than seventy fighting men, not counting all the workers and servants. But as soon as the raiders came, they made such a fierce attack that they shook the gates and hacked at the door-posts, so that the latches and bolts on the inside of the gates gave way. The king's men fell back, and the raiders forced their way inside. Then a great battle broke out. So says Starkad:

> So we came
> to the king's fort.
> We shook the gates,
> we smashed the posts,
> we broke the bars,
> we brandished swords.
> On the king's side
> there stood against us
> seventy heroes
> of high degree.
> All the thralls
> were there as well,
> laboring men
> and luggers of water.

Tale of King Vikar

King Herthjof defended himself for a long time with his forces, because he had many brave men, but since Vikar had chosen brave champions for his forces, King Herthjof's men fell back before them. Vikar was always in the forefront of his men. So said Starkad:

> 'Twas in vain, to advance
> by Vikar' side,
> for first and foremost
> of fighters he stood;
> we hewed helmets
> and heads' crowns,
> slashing byrnies
> and splintering shields.

Starkad fiercely attacked King Herthjof, along with Vikar, and they gave him his death. All of Vikar's champions attacked fiercely. Many men fell there, but some were wounded. So said Starkad:

> Vikar was fated
> for victory,
> but deadly strife
> was destined for Herthjof.
> We struck soldiers,
> some we killed;
> I wasn't far from
> the fall of the king.

Vikar had the victory there, but King Herthjof fell, as was said before, and thirty men with him. Many were fatally wounded. But none of Vikar's men fell.

After that, Vikar took all the ships that King Herthjof had owned, and all the forces which he had assembled. At once he went eastward along the coast with all the men who would follow him. When he came to Agder, those who had been friends of his father came to him. Soon he had a great multitude following him. Then he was raised to the kingship over all Agder and Jaederen, and he laid Hordaland and Hardanger under his rule, and all the kingdom that King Herthjof had had.

King Vikar soon became mighty, and the greatest of warriors. He went raiding every summer. King Vikar went with his host eastward, into the Oslofjord, and landed on the east side of the fjord, and raided in Gautland and accomplished many brave deeds there. But when he came up to Lake Vänern, the king named Sisar came against him. He was from the east, from Kiev. He was a great champion and had large forces. King Vikar and Sisar had a fierce battle there, and Sisar advanced fiercely and killed many men in King Vikar's ranks.

Starkad was there with King Vikar. He advanced against Sisar, and they exchanged blows for a long time, and neither one had any reason to doubt the strength of the other's blows. Sisar knocked away Starkad's shield, and gave him two great wounds in his head with his sword and broke his collarbone. Starkad was also wounded above the hip, on his side. So says Starkad:

> You weren't with Vikar
> on Vänern lake
> off in the east,
> early that day,
> when we sought Sisar
> on the slaughter-field,
> a more strenuous deed
> than it seems to you.
>
> He let his blade,
> bitterly sharp,
> skewer my shield
> and sorely wound me,
> cutting helm from head
> and hitting my skull;
> my cheek and jaw
> he chopped to the molars,
> leaving broken
> my left collarbone.

Starkad also took a deep wound in the other side from the thrusting-spear that Sisar fought with. So said Starkad:

> And in my side,
> the strong fighter
> bit with his blade
> above my hip.
> He stabbed his spear
> in my other side;
> the icy point
> penetrated deeply.
> They still may see
> my scars, now healed.

Starkad struck Sisar with his sword and sliced through his side, and gave him a great wound in his leg below the knee, and in the end he cut off his other foot at the ankle, and then King Sisar fell. So says Starkad:

> On his other side
> I sliced him up,
> broke his body
> with biting edge;
> I swung my sword
> in the struggle's heat,
> all my power
> I put forth there.

In the battle, both sides suffered great losses, but King Vikar won the victory, and the surviving Kievans turned and fled. After this victory, Vikar went home to his kingdom.

CHAPTER V

King Vikar heard that King Geirthjof had summoned large forces in Oppland, meaning to attack King Vikar with that host and avenge King Herthjof, his brother. Then King Vikar called up the levy from his kingdom, and he went with those forces to Oppland to oppose King Geirthjof. They had such a great battle that they fought continuously for seventeen days. King Geirthjof fell, and King Vikar had the victory.

Then King Vikar won Oppland and Telemark for his own, because King Fridthjof of Telemark was away from his own kingdom. Starkad states that the battle which King Vikar won in Oppland was his third battle:

> For the third time
> the thewful one
> held a contest
> of Hild's game°,   *Hild*: a valkyrie; *Hild's game*: war
> before Oppland
> was finally won
> and Geirthjof
> was given to Hel.°   *Hel*: goddess of the realm of the dead

At once Vikar set men to rule the kingdom which he had won in Oppland. He went home to Agder and became a powerful king with a large following. He married a wife and had two sons with her. The older was named Harald, and the younger was named Neri. Neri was the wisest of men, and everything he set his mind to turned out well, but he was so stingy that he could not give anything away without regretting it at once. So said Starkad:

> The great king
> begat for himself
> two sons and heirs,
> splendid men.
> His elder son,
> Harald by name,
> was established
> as Telemark's lord.
>
> It's said that Jarl Neri
> was a stingy man
> with gold, though giving
> goodly counsel.
> Vikar's son,
> seasoned in battle,

was sole ruler
of the shire of Oppland.

Jarl Neri was a great warrior, but so stingy that all the stingiest men have been compared to him, and since then his name has been given to others. But when Fridthjof heard of the fall of his brothers, he went to Oppland and conquered the kingdom that Vikar had previously won. Then he sent word to Vikar that he should pay him tribute from his kingdom, or else be invaded. So said Starkad:

> Fridthjof chose
> first to send
> a war-message
> to the wise leader:
> would Vikar suffer
> invading foes,
> or pay the prince
> the price of tribute.

When this message came to Vikar, he summoned the assembly and discussed with his counselors how to answer this difficult question. They all put forth their counsel and deliberated for a long time. So said Starkad:

> We took counsel,
> discussed it long,
> soon we became
> stirred to anger;
> the host chose
> that the hardy king
> should press on
> with the promised battle.

They sent word to King Frithjof that King Vikar would defend his land. Then King Fridthjof went with his host and intended to harry King Vikar.

Sagas of Fridthjof

Olaf the Keen-Eyed was the name of a king in Sweden, at the place which is called Närke. He was mighty and a great warrior. He summoned the levy from his own kingdom and went to aid King Vikar. They had a huge force and went with it against King Fridthjof, and they arranged their forces for battle in the boar's-head formation[4]. So said Starkad:

> Olaf the Keen-Eyed,
> king most favored,
> was sovereign lord
> of Sweden in the east;
> he called out
> the kingdom's levy;
> his share of troops
> was said to be large.

There a fierce battle began, and King Vikar's men boldly advanced, for there were many champions in the ranks with them. The foremost champion was Starkad Storvirksson. Others were Ulf and Erp, and many other good warriors and great champions. King Vikar fiercely advanced forward. Starkad was unarmored and went through the ranks and struck with both hands, as is said here:

> We went forward
> in the weapon-clash°,   *weapon-clash*: battle
> the king's men
> were keen for battle;
> Ulf was seen there,
> Erp as well;
> stripped of armor,
> I struck with both hands.

And when King Vikar attacked King Fridthjof fiercely with his champions, his ranks were on the verge of breaking up. Then he begged King Vikar for peace. So said Starkad:

> Fridthjof decided
> to sue for peace,

> since Vikar refused
> to fall back,
> and Storvirk's son,
> Starkad himself,
> attacked fiercely
> before everyone.

There was the greatest battle and the sharpest, and the greater part of King Fridthjof's forces fell. But when he begged for peace, King Vikar stood down his host.

Then King Fridthjof came to a settlement with King Vikar. King Olaf had to arrange a settled agreement between them, and it was so arranged that King Fridthjof gave up all his rule over Oppland and Telemark, and he left the land. Vikar set his own sons over this kingdom. He gave Harald the title of king over Telemark, but to Neri he gave the title of jarl and the rulership of Oppland. He became friends with King Gautrek in Gautland, and it is said in some books that Neri held some of his realm from King Gautrek, that portion of Gautland which was closest to him, and he was also a jarl of King Gautrek and advised him whenever it was necessary. After that, King Vikar went home to his kingdom and became very famous from his victories, and he and King Olaf parted in friendship and held to their friendship ever after. Olaf went east, to his home in Sweden.

[Chapter VI belongs to the next section of *Gautreks saga*, known as *Gjafa-Refs páttr*. *Víkars páttr* resumes with Chapter VII.]

CHAPTER VII

King Vikar became a great warrior and had many famous champions with him, but Starkad was the most valued of them all and dearest to the king, where he was his highest-ranking liegeman and counselor and defender of his lands. He received many gifts from the king. King Vikar gave him a goodly ring that weighed three marks, and Starkad gave the king the island of Thruma, which King Harald had granted to Storvirk, his father. He was with King Vikar for fifteen summers, as he said:

> Vikar gifted me
> with gold from afar,
> this red ring,
> which rides on my hand,
> three marks in weight,
> and Thruma I gave him.
> I fared in his forces
> for fifteen summers.

King Vikar sailed from Ogd northwards to Hordaland, and he had a great host. He anchored in certain islands for a long time, but got strong headwinds. They cast wood-chips[5] for a favorable wind, and the omens showed that Odin wanted to claim a man from the host to be hanged, to be chosen by drawing lots. Then the host was assembled for the drawing of lots, and King Vikar's lot came up. Everyone fell silent at this, and it was planned that the counselors should have a meeting about this difficult question on the next day.

That night, around midnight, Horsehair-Grani awakened Starkad, his foster-son, and told him to go with him. They took a small boat and rowed to an island nearby. They went up into the forest and found a clearing there. In the clearing were a great many people, and an assembly was seated there. Eleven men were sitting on chairs, and the twelfth was empty.[6] They went forward to the assembly, and Horsehair-Grani sat down on the twelfth chair. They all greeted him as Odin. He said that the judges should then set the destiny of Starkad.

Then Thor began to speak, and he said, "Alfhild, the mother of Starkad's father, chose a cunning giant as the father of her son, rather than Asa-Thor. I shape Starkad's fate so that he shall never have a son nor a daughter, and so his lineage shall come to an end."

Odin answered, "I shape his fate so that he shall live three human lifetimes."

Thor said, "He shall accomplish a vile deed in each lifetime."

Odin answered, "I shape his fate so that he shall own the best weapons and clothes."

Thor said, "I shape his fate so that he shall never own land nor estates."

Odin said, "I grant him this: that he shall have abundance of money."

Thor said, "I lay this fate upon him: he shall never think that he has enough."

Odin answered, "I give him victory and prowess in every battle."

Thor answered, "I lay this fate upon him: in every battle he shall receive a disfiguring wound."

Odin said, "I give him the art of poetry, so that he shall compose poetry as fast as he can recite it."[7]

Thor said, "He shall not remember what he has composed."

Odin said, "I shape this fate for him: he shall seem highest to the noblest and best men."

Thor said, "He shall be loathed by all the common folk."

Then the judges passed sentence that everything that Odin and Thor had spoken should befall Starkad, and so the assembly broke up. Starkad and Horsehair-Grani went to their boat. Then Horsehair-Grani said to Starkad, "Now you can repay me well, foster-son, for the help that I have given you."

"It is well," said Starkad.

Horsehair-Grani said, "Then you must now send King Vikar to me, and I will give you the plan."

Starkad agreed to this. Then Horsehair-Grani put a spear in his hand, and said that it would appear to be a reed sprout. They went out to their men as day was breaking.

The next morning, the king's advisors assembled for deliberation. It was agreed that they had to do some sort of representation of the sacrifice, and Starkad told them his plan. There stood a fir-tree next to them, and a single high stump next to the fir. Low on the fir tree there was a narrow branch, and it extended up to the crown of the tree. Then the serving-men prepared food for the men, and a calf was butchered and gutted. Starkad had them take the calf's intestines, and he stepped up on the stump and bent the slender branch down and tied the calf's intestines around it.

Then Starkad said to the king, "Now a gallows is prepared for you, king, and it shouldn't seem very dangerous. Now come here, and I'll place a noose around your neck."

The king said, "Should this device be no more dangerous than it looks, I suppose that it won't harm me. But if it's otherwise, then fate

Sagas of Fridthjof

must decide what happens."

Then he stepped up on the stump, and Starkad laid the noose around his neck and then stepped down from the stump. Then Starkad stabbed at the king with the reed and said, "Now I give you to Odin."

Then Starkad let the fir-branch loose. The reed-sprout became a spear and pierced the king through.[8] The stump fell from under his feet, and the calf's intestines became strong withies, and the branch sprang up and hoisted the king into the crown of the tree, and he died there. Since then, that place is called Vikar's Island.[9]

Starkad became much abhorred by all the people, and for this deed he was first exiled from Hordaland. After that, he fled Norway and went east to Sweden, and stayed for a long time with the kings at Uppsala, Eirek and Alrek the sons of Agni Skjalf's Husband, and he went on raids with them. And when Alrek asked Starkad what news he could tell them about his kinsmen or about himself, Starkad made the poem that is called "Vikar's Piece". Thus he told of the killing of King Vikar:

> I fared with the troops,
> the finest I knew,
> in all my life
> I liked this the best,
> before we fared
> one final time
> to Hordaland,
> haunted by trolls.
>
> It was on this foray
> that Thor fated for me
> a mean reputation
> and manifold hardships;
> I, the base one,
> was bound to wreak ill.
>
> Among high trees
> I had to consecrate
> Geirthjof's Bane
> to the gods, King Vikar.

Tale of King Vikar

I stabbed the sovereign
with a spear in the heart,
the most dismal deed
ever done by my hands.

From there I wandered
on winding roads,
hated in Hordaland,
my heart sorrowing,
lacking in rings
and lays of brave deeds,
deprived of my prince,
despairing in mind.

Now I have sought out
the Swedish realm,
and Uppsala,
the Ynglings' seat;
the lord's own sons,
as I'll long remember,
say that I sit
as a silent thul[10].

Concerning Starkad, it may be seen that he thought that his worst and most monstrous deed was that he killed King Vikar, and we have not heard stories that he settled down in Norway afterwards. But when Starkad was at Uppsala, there were twelve berserk mercenaries there. They treated him scornfully and mocked him, and the two brothers Ulf and Otrygg were the most vehement at that. Starkad was silent, but the berserks called him a reborn giant and a worthless man, as is said here:

Among the lads
they let me sit,
greatly scorned,
snowy-browed;
the high ones mock me,
the haughty men

make the lord's creature
a laughing-stock.

On me myself
they imagine they see
the marks of eight
arms of a giant,
which Hlorridi° tore   *Hlorridi*: the god Thor
from Hergrim's Bane,
ripped with his hands
on rocks in the north.[11]

The warriors laugh
to look at me,
my loathsome mug
and long snout,
wolf-hoary hair,
hands all gnarled,
scabby neck
and scaly hide.

When King Eirek and Alrek set out for home, Starkad went on a raid with the ship that King Eirek had given him, crewed with Norwegians and Danes. He traveled far and wide to many lands and engaged in battles and single combats, and always won victories, and he is no longer in this saga.

    King Alrek didn't live long, and that happened in this way: King Eirek his brother knocked him into Hel with a bridle, when they had ridden out to tame their horses.[12] After that, King Eirek ruled Sweden alone for a long time, as will be told later, in the saga of Hrolf Gautreksson and his shipmates.

APPENDIX:
THE SHORTER SAGA OF FRIDTHJOF THE BOLD

CHAPTER I

There once was a king named Beli, who ruled over the realm of Sogn. He had two sons and one daughter. One of his sons was named Helgi, and the other was Halfdan. His daughter was named Ingibjorg. She was beautiful and wise, and in every respect the foremost of the king's children. King Beli's queen had died. A short distance away, on the west side of the fjord, was a place that they called Balder's Meadow. It was a sanctuary and a great temple.

Ingibjorg the king's daughter was fostered by a man named Hilding. He was a wealthy farmer.

Thorstein was the name of a famous man who lived in Sogn. His son was named Fridthjof. He was the most handsome of men and the best at sports, and far ahead of the king's sons. Fridthjof was always with Hilding, and he and the king's daughter were foster-siblings. They greatly surpassed other people.

Two men are named in this saga. One was named Bjorn, and the other was Asmund. They were not of high birth. They were Fridthjof's sworn brothers and well-disposed toward him. The king was not wealthy in treasure, but the hersir Thorstein held a third of the kingdom and had to take charge of the land's defenses on behalf of the king. He held a feast for the king every third year, and they were the most magnificent of feasts.

King Beli became sick and called his sons to him and said: "This illness will carry me off from my kingdom, and from my life as well. I want to ask you two to keep the friends which I have had before, because you seem to me to come up short in every way, compared to Thorstein and his son. They will be steadfast friends, if you treat them well. You must not put riches into my burial mound next to me. My mound shall stand

Appendix: Shorter Saga of Fridthjof

next to the fjord. But Thorstein's and mine will be a short distance apart, and it will be good for us to call to each other." And then he died.

Then Thorstein became ill, and he said, "I will ask this of you, Fridthjof, that you restrain your temper around the king's sons, even though you are no less worthy than them, because it has to be so for the sake of their rank. My heart tells me that this will turn out well." Then he died, and he was buried in a mound, across from Beli's mound.

It was Bjorn whom Fridthjof esteemed the most, and Asmund served them. Fridthjof had a ship which was called Ellidi. Another one of his possessions was a ring; no other was like it. It was rumored that Fridthjof seemed no less noble than the king's sons, except for their kingly rank. People found out that there was great love between the king's daughter and Fridthjof. The king's sons found out about it and didn't like it at all, and there was coldness between them and Fridthjof.

Now it happened that the king's sons had to attend the feast, and it went ahead in great splendor. Fridthjof often talked with Ingibjorg the king's daughter. "You have a good ring", she said.

He answered, "I don't have what I haven't earned."

She answered: "That's what people say: only he who is living, not dead, has wealth."

He answered: "You have the choice to own the ring and not part with it. Send it back to me, if you hate having it."

She answered, "You shall have in exchange the ring which I have", and so it was.

After that, they parted. Fridthjof now was taciturn. His sworn brother Bjorn asked what was wrong.

He answered: "I have marriage on my mind. Though it would be a match far above my station, I am no less worthy in my bearing."

Bjorn said: "Why shouldn't we go and put forth this suit?"

They went right away. The kings were sitting on their father's mound. Fridthjof greeted them and said, "This is my errand to you: I want to ask for your sister in marriage."

They answered, "To give her to a man of no rank is not a worthy request to make. We don't intend for her to be given to a man with no standing."

He answered, "Then I can tell you right away that I will never provide you with support."

"We'll never care about that," they said.

Fridthjof came home afterwards, and became cheerful again.

CHAPTER II

There was a king named Hring who ruled over Sweden. He once spoke privately with his friends: "I have heard that the sons of King Beli have severed their friendship with Fridthjof, who is the most excellent of all of them. Now I will send my men to meet with them, so that they may submit to me, or else I will raise a host against them. It will be easy to conquer them, because neither of them is a match for me, neither in strength nor in cleverness, and it's good to overcome them in my old age."

The messengers came to Beli's sons and spoke these words: "The King of Swedes sends this message to you, and wishes for you to yield tribute to him, or else fight with him." They said that they did not wish to serve him in their youth, in shame and disgrace, and the messengers went back with their words to their king.

The king's sons summoned their forces, but they got a small host. They sent word to Fridthjof and asked for his support. He was sitting at a board-game[1] when the messengers came to him. They said: "Our kings send you greetings, and they wish to accept your assistance in the battle alongside them."

He didn't answer and said to Bjorn: "Come up with a plan for your play, for there are two alternatives before you, two ways to play."

Then the messengers said: "Did you hear what we said?"

Fridthjof answered them, and he said that he had heard them for a long time—"but I will never assist them."

Then the messengers returned and told how it had gone to the brothers. After that, the brothers prepared for their journey, and gave the order to bring their sister to Balder's Meadow, along with eight serving-women, "because no one is so foolhardy that he would damage it". For there was a great temple with sacrifices to the gods, and a plank fence around the temple. Women and men could not meet together there.

The king's sons went to battle against King Hring, as was said before. As soon as both kings had gone away, Fridthjof told his men to launch the ship Ellida—"and we'll find out whether it can sail to Balder's Meadow."

Now they came there and were welcomed warmly. Fridthjof sat down next to the king's daughter, and all his men arranged their seats. The king's daughter said: "You've got some nerve, Fridthjof, since you want to sail a ship with a crew of fourteen here to Balder's Meadow."

He answered: "I never cared about Balder or your sacrifices. Conversing with you is just as good to me, here or at home."

There was no shortage of drink and good cheer. So it went on every day, while the kings were away, that they went there and enjoyed themselves.

CHAPTER III

Now there is this to say about the king's dealings: they found that King Hring had a much larger force than the brothers. Friends of both of them went between them and asked them to make a settlement. King Hring said, "Will the kings put themselves under my authority and give me their sister in marriage and give her wealth, as befits her well?" Because the kings had few men, they agreed to this, and they bound it with oaths. They parted company with their friends, and the brothers went home.

Now it's time to tell about Fridthjof. He said to the king's daughter, "You have given us a fine welcome, but I must go home for now. But if the kings have come home, they'll find out what you've done for us, one way or another."

The king's daughter replied, "You haven't heeded their warning. But certainly we have to welcome our friends, if you come back."

After that they went home, and in the morning Fridthjof went outside and said, "Now it may be, Bjorn my comrade, that our pleasure-journeys to Balder's Meadow are hindered."

Now the kings came home and heard what had happened while they were away. They became very angry and said that a great disgrace had been done to them. Then friends came between them and asked Fridthjof to give some compensation to the kings. He said, "The only thing I will grant, for my part, is an agreement to keep the peace as a remembrance of our forebears. But we will not show them any faithfulness."

Then the messengers said: "The kings wish to accept this as a settlement: that you fetch home the tribute from jarl Angantyr, who rules over Orkney, because that tribute has long been neglected."

Fridthjof said, "Then we want our property to be left in peace," and that was promised to him. Right away, Fridthjof and thirteen of his men made the ship Ellidi ready.

It was intended that King Hring would fetch the king's daughter in the autumn. And when Fridthjof had gone away, Helgi said, "It would be best, brother, for Fridthjof to suffer punishment. We two will burn his farm." Then they burned the farmstead at Framnes. After that, they paid sorcerous women so that they might call down a fierce storm on Fridthjof and his men.

Now when they had gone a short distance from land, the sea grew unquiet, and a great storm blew up. Then Fridthjof spoke a verse:

> In former days
> in Framnes,
> I oft manned the oars
> to meet Ingibjorg.
> Now I shall sail
> in the stiff breeze,
> let the swift sea-beast
> surge beneath me.

"And now is our chance", he said, "to test good sailors. But it would be more enjoyable to be in Balder's Meadow."

Bjorn said: "It's to be expected that we will come back, and we will be glad of it."

Just then the ship was heavily swamped, but they kept up their spirits excellently, because they were all gathered together with good companions. Then Fridthjof spoke this verse:

> Swells can't be seen
> as we sail westwards.
> All the ocean seems to me
> like embers stirring.

Appendix: Shorter Saga of Fridthjof

> Sea-billows are streaming,
> swan's land° throws up mounds.　　　　　*swan's land:* sea
> Now Ellidi tosses
> on terrible breakers.

Bjorn said, "That's true, foster-brother. Nothing's gone wrong yet, though the waves rattle on the boards." And then Fridthjof spoke a verse.

> If in the swan's slopes°　　　　　*swan's slopes:* sea
> I must sink deep,
> the maid will mourn me
> and drink much to me—
> bilge-water surges
> are swamping Ellidi—
> although the linens
> lay, somewhat bleached.

Bjorn said, "I've just remembered. Do you think that the maidens of Sogn will shed many tears for you?"

He answered, "It's crossed my mind."

Just then the storm became so great that torrents fell into the ship on both sides. Then Bjorn spoke a verse:

> It's not as if some dame
> in the east toasts our fame,
> or bids you be bolder,
> that bright rings' holder.°　　　　　*ring's holder:* woman
> Salty are the eyes
> if briny seas rise.
> Strong arms give way,
> eyes sting from spray.

Fridthjof said: "So it will seem to you. It will test us in different ways." Then Asmund spoke a verse:

> There was a struggle with the sail
> as the sea crashed over me.
> I must labor in this longship
> alone, with eight others.
> It's better, bringing breakfast
> to the bowers of the ladies,
> than baling water from Ellidi
> as the breakers splash.[2]

Then Fridthjof said, "You just now showed that you're descended from thralls." Fridthjof said:

> I sat on a bolster
> in Balder's Meadow,
> sang what I could
> for the king's daughter.
> Now I will rest on
> Ran's trusty bed,
> while another lies
> by lady Ingibjorg.

Bjorn said, "Now these are strong words, sworn brother. You never spoke in such a way that there was fear in your words."

Fridthjof answered, "It's not certain that that didn't come into my mind just now." He said:

> I paid the price for these trips,
> when proud Ingibjorg came
> to meet me—but not you—
> with eight maids-in-waiting.
> We placed pure gold rings together,
> pledged troth in Balder's Meadow;
> the keeper of Halfdan's enclosure°   *keeper of H's enclosure:* Balder
> was not close at hand that day.

Bjorn said: "We must be content with what's been done, sworn brother."

Appendix: Shorter Saga of Fridthjof

And with that there came such a great wave crashing over the ship, that the gunwales were torn loose, and four men perished. Then Fridthjof said: "Now it is certain that we shall go to Ran, and we shall prepare ourselves bravely. Everyone shall have gold on himself and break apart the ring, Ingibjorg's Gift, and we will divide it amongst ourselves." And then he spoke a verse:

> Now the sea
> has stripped away
> four of our sailors,
> who should have lived.
> But Ran will receive
> resolute warriors,
> that savage woman,
> with a seat and bed.

Bjorn said: "It's not so hopeless, even if it doesn't appear hopeful." Then Fridthjof spoke:

> And so the red-gold ring
> of the rich father of Halfdan
> must be broken, before
> Ægir blots us out.
> He'll see gold on his guests,
> if good lodging we need,
> which helps splendid heroes
> in the hall of Ran.

Now they found that the ship was skimming quickly, but they didn't know where they had come to. Fridthjof immediately went up in the mast and came back down and said: "I saw a very strange sight just now. A whale is swimming in a ring around our ship. I expect that we have land near us, and I guess that it wants to block us from landing. I think that Helgi and Halfdan have not dealt with us in a friendly way, and they must have sent us no friendly message. I saw two women on the back of the whale, blocking our course. Now we will find out which may be greater, our luck or their sorcery, and we will steer right at them." And then he spoke a verse:

> I see two troll-women
> on the tossing waves;
> Helgi has had them
> sent hither to us.
> Ellidi's keel shall
> cleave them asunder,
> rip them into pieces,
> before reaching land.

At once he encouraged his men heartily, and it so happened that, by his valor, they broke the spine and legs of the two shape-shifters. Just then the sea calmed, and the ship bobbed back up, and they had come to land. But those who had survived had been so hard-pressed that Fridthjof carried them all to land, except that Bjorn alone managed to save himself. Fridthjof spread the sail on them and spoke a verse:

> I hauled eight
> exhausted warriors
> to the hearth-fire
> in howling winds.
> Now I've spread the sail
> out on the sand;
> it's not easy to struggle
> against the sea's might.

And then he said:

> We've no need, warriors,
> to worry about death.
> Be most happy,
> my heroes all!
> If my dreams tell it,
> true it must be

that I will marry
Ingibjorg.

Bjorn said: "Still she comes into your mind. It's calm now, and you are behaving like a man."

A short way from there was the seat of Jarl Angantyr. It had just happened that a man named Hallvard was drinking his penalty horn[3], and he had to sit through the night in the hall, facing the wind. He held the horn in his hand as he sat there, and could see the travelers, and spoke a verse:

> No shelter for drinking
> outside the hall
> for western Vikings,
> as would be within.
> Those are mighty
> men, who are baling
> the roller-horse°
> in the raging storm.

roller-horse: ship

And he also said:

> I see six baling,
> and seven rowing,
> weary warriors
> in the windstorm.
> One like Fridthjof,
> fearless in war,
> is perched in the prow
> and pulls at the oars.

Then he went to the cup-bearers and spoke a verse:

> Pick up off the floor
> this overturned horn!
> I've drunk it all down,
> delicate lady.

> I see storm-worn
> sailing men—
> I must help them
> to make harbor.

The jarl said, "What is the news?"

"Lord", he said, "men are drawing up on land, and I think they are good warriors."

The jarl said, "Go out to meet them, if Fridthjof has come here, who is the most famous one."

There was a viking named Atli. They were twelve all together. He said: "I have been told that Fridthjof has sworn an oath that he will not be the first to beg for peace. Now it's time to put that to the test, if he's come here."

Hallvard said that putting them to the test was uncalled for. Then they came to where Fridthjof had awakened, because he had become rather sleepy. Atli said, "Now it's advisable, Fridthjof, to behave well and test the old saying that eagles claw each other when face to face, although you must not think that you need to ask for peace." Fridthjof spoke a verse:

> You can't keep us
> cowering here,
> you fear-filled,
> freakish islanders.
> I'd rather dare
> ten dreadful foes,
> standing alone,
> than sue for peace.
> of ten of you.

Then Hallvard came up and said, "Stop this talk. All of them are welcome here, as our jarl wills, and you shall go to the hall."

Fridthjof said that he would like that very much, but yet he felt that either was worthy, peace or war.

Hallvard said, "I have managed to hear of you, and we are truly well-met. You have been put through such a trial."

After that they went to the hall. Fridthjof went before the jarl and greeted him. The jarl welcomed him nobly and asked him about his voyage, and he told all, most truly. The jarl said, "Evil may be expected from such kings as Helgi, and both the brothers are of no account, but they confront such brave men with such evil." Bjorn spoke a verse:

> We blithe ones baled
> as cold waves broke
> over both sides
> for eighteen days.
> That's how this wise
> warband travels,
> that's how we fare
> with Fridthjof.

Now they were all received warmly.

Fridthjof became gloomy. The jarl said, "Why are you so silent, Fridthjof, since we want to do well for you? And if you've come to fetch tribute, then I have a quick answer: the kings will get no tribute and no good portion from us, for they have been no good to us. But you shall get whatever you ask for, and do what you like with the money. I don't fear them."

"I will accept that," said Fridthjof, and he was there in good favor next to the jarl.

CHAPTER IV

Now there is to say about that, that King Hring came to the feast and went to his own wedding, and it had happened that the sorcerous women had fallen off their platform.[4] And when the feast was ended, King Hring saw the ring Fridthjof's Gift on Ingibjorg's hand, and said, "How did you come to have that ring?"

She said that it was her heirloom.

"No," he said, "rather, Fridthjof must have given it to you. You shall not have his gold, because you will get gold in my kingdom."

Then she put the ring in the hand of Helgi's wife and begged her to send it to Fridthjof, as they had agreed. After that, the king went home to his kingdom, and Ingibjorg with him.

But Fridthjof prepared to leave Orkney, and the jarl had his ship repaired. Jarl Angantyr and Fridthjof separated with the greatest joy. Then they returned to Norway and into Sognefjord, and they came before the estate that Fridthjof had had. Then he said, "Now the settlements have been charred, while we have been away." He now spoke with his men, and they were all glad to see him, and they told him the kings' designs. Then he spoke a verse:

> Daring companions
> all drank together
> with my father
> at Framnes, once.
> Now I see the farm
> by flames burned.
> I must repay
> the princes' evil.

He then asked them where the kings were, and he was told that they were in Balder's Meadow, and were sacrificing to their god.

Then Fridthjof spoke: "What appears to you, Bjorn," he said, "how it shall go?"

Bjorn said, "I'll let you make a plan for us".

"Then I intend to bring them their tribute, however it is discharged." And so they did, and they left the ship.

Fridthjof said to Bjorn, "We two will go up onto land, but in the meantime the others shall break the kings' ships, because I will only pay their tribute, which isn't likely, if it seems to us the same way for all." Then Fridthjof spoke a verse:

> I will go alone
> up from the shore
> to find the king—
> I crave no help.
> You, fling fire into
> this fighter's house,

> if I've not returned
> before twilight.

Bjorn said, "Well spoken."

The kings sat in the house of their gods, and their wives were warming the idols by the fire. At that moment, Fridthjof went before Helgi and said, "You'll want to have your tribute now," and brought up the purse and slammed it into his nose and knocked out two of his teeth. Helgi fell unconscious, but Fridthjof went to the fires and saw the ring on the hand of Helgi's wife. He grabbed her, and she was dragged along, but the idol rolled into the fire, and when he came to the doors, he pulled the ring off her hand. Fridthjof came out and spoke a verse:

> Accept this tribute,
> o stately lord!
> Take it in your teeth,
> don't you trouble us further.
> The silver is down in
> this sack's bottom,
> as Bjorn and I have
> both offered you.

After that Fridthjof went out and spoke a verse:

> I must take the ring
> of red gold in hand
> from the sleeping-quarters
> of Svolnir's maids.[5]
> My heart claims this prize
> from the pudgy ones:
> it gave little good
> to its guardians.

Bjorn said, "Now you've arranged things well; she stayed behind, but you've got the ring." Then they went to the ships, and Fridthjof looked back and spoke a verse:

I got away from the garth
of two green-earth's rulers,[6]
so that I might not suffer
from slander and rumors.
Oft I was noticed next to
the Gunn of needle and pin°—   *Gunn*: a valkyrie;
that forced me to flee my home—   *Gunn of needle and pin*: woman
more frequently than I should.

Helgi came to his senses and ordered men to go out—"and that man who did not spare the sanctuary has forfeited his life." And when they came out, he ordered them to fetch him his bow, but when he bent the bow, the bow broke apart. Fridthjof spoke a verse when he saw that, as he stepped onto the ship and took the oars and broke both with one pull:

I kissed the young
Ingibjorg,
Beli's daughter,
in Balder's Meadow.
So the oars
on Ellidi
shall both break
like the bow of Helgi.

Then the kings went to their ships, but they were all broken.

Now Bjorn said to Fridthjof, "What shall we do for a living now, sworn brother?"

"I suppose it's now advisable," said Fridthjof, "to learn the warrior's way and take up raiding." And so they did, they took up raiding for a time, and Fridthjof became a bold man. He killed wicked men, but he let farmers live in peace, and from this they became very wealthy.

CHAPTER V

It is said that at one time, Fridthjof said to Bjorn, "Now I am tired of this occupation. I now intends to separate from you, and I want to meet

Appendix: Shorter Saga of Fridthjof

King Hring, but visit me again in the summer."

Bjorn said, "That plan has little hope of success, yet you must decide. Don't you want to return and kill the kings?"

Fridthjof said that would not happen, and spoke a verse:

> I don't remember
> the mild countenance
> of Beli's daughter
> in Balder's Meadow.
> So I must seek Hring
> to speak with him,
> to find how the folk-ruler
> favors warriors.

"I am unwilling," said Bjorn, "for you to risk going alone into his power." He said that he wanted to decide—"and convey me there," and so they did.

When he came near the settlement, he took a long salt-maker's cowl and threw it over himself. He was a greatly grown man and tall, handsome to see. Then he met some shepherds, and went up to them shyly and asked where they were. They said that they were in front of the home of King Hring.

He asked, "Is he a mighty king?"

They answered, "It seems to us that you must be old enough to use your wits to realize what might King Hring has."

He answered: "I have thought more about polishing the salt-kettle than asking about the glories of kings." Then he went to the hall and came in and took a place on the edge, by the door.

The king said when he saw the man: "My queen, a man has come into the hall."

The queen answered, "Here that is small news."

"Certainly," he said. "Go, boy, and ask who he is, where he has come from, and where his kinfolk live."

The boy came up to him and asked, "What is your name, what kin do you come of, and where were you last night?"

He answered, "You're quick to ask. Will you be able to use any discernment if I tell you? I am called Thief, and I was with Wolf in the night, and I was raised in Straits."

The boy told that to the king and queen. "You understand well," said the king. "I know the district called Straits, and being in Straits may not often ease the minds of most men. It may also be that his name is shortened, and that he has been with untrustworthy men for a while. The man appears quite worthy to me."

"What is the worth of a beggar?", said the queen.

The king said, "I am curious to see him. I see that he thinks much and looks around."

Then the king sent for him, and he came before the king. The king said, "What is the name of such a tall man?"

He said the same.

The king said, "So it may be. How do you wish, queen, to welcome him?"

She answered, "Like other beggars."

"No," said the king, "he must have been in the forest at night, since he said that he spent the night with Wolf, and he must need hospitality. Sit here between me and the queen."

She said, "You've become senile, since you arrange seating for salt-boilers."

The king said, "That is not your affair. Throw off your cowl, Thief."

He said that wouldn't be fitting—"and I'm a shy man."

The king said, "Do as I bid. I will decide."

Then he took off the cowls, and the man was exceptionally handsome.

"Now I call it better to go and get him a proper mantle," said the king.

She said that it would be so—"but I don't think much of him."

The king said, "You have a good ring, Thief, and you must have been boiling salt for a long time to get it."

He said that it was an inheritance from his father.

The king said, "That may be."

Then the king sat down in the high seat, but the queen blushed as red as blood and didn't want to have anything to do with him, but the king was quite happy, and he was able to talk with him much, and he was liked well by men, and he was treated with great honor through the winter. The queen spoke little with him.

It happened once that the king had to go to a feast, and then the king said, "Will you come with us, Thief?"

"Yes, lord," he answered.

Then they went, and the king and queen had driven out onto the ice. Thief said, "Go carefully, because the ice is treacherous."

The king said, "It's often that we're on your mind."

And a moment later the ice broke, but Thief rushed at the wagons and he saved the king and queen and everything that was in the wagon, but the queen was behind, and he snatched her up out of the crack in the ice. The king said, "Well were we helped. Fridthjof could not have done better had he been standing nearby, and men like you are good retainers."

Now the fair spring came, and one day the king said: "Let us two go out now by day and look around. Here is a fair landscape."

Then the two of them went together, the king and Thief, and they came into a forest. The king said, "I'm getting sleepy now."

Thief said, "Go home instead, lord. That is more suitable to your dignity."

"No," said the king, "that may not be," and he lay down and began snoring loudly. Thief sat nearby and drew his sword from its scabbard and flung it far away, but the king awakened and said, "Was it so, Fridthjof, that various things came into your mind? You shall be welcome here, and I recognized you from the first evening I saw you. And you must not go away so quickly. Something great lies in store you."

He answered, "Well and nobly have you dealt with me, but now we must go away quickly." After that they went home.

And in the morning there was a knocking at the door of the king's chamber. He asked who was there. "It's Fridthjof, and now I intend to go." And then he spoke a verse:

> Now I must give you great thanks.
> You granted a magnificent—
> this poet's prepared to leave—
> place to this feeder of eagles.°

feeder of eagles: warrior

> I will remember Ingibjorg
> always, while we two live—
> stay well!—but we are fated
> to furnish treasures, not kisses.

The king said: "And it's true that you thanked her for help better than you thanked me. She has not done better to you than I. Let us have a meal all together before you go, and let's be cheerful. Sit up, my queen."

She said that she didn't feel like it.

"No," said the king, "we must all have food together,", and so it was done.

The king said, "I want you to stay here, Fridthjof."

Fridthjof spoke a verse, first saying "I mean to go away now."

> King Hring, live
> hale and long,
> highest overlord
> under Ymir's skull.
> Keep well, ruler,
> your wife and lands,
> I shall never see
> Ingibjorg again.

Then the king said:

> Don't depart from here,
> dearest of warriors,
> don't flee, Fridthjof,
> with fretful heart.
> I will grant you
> gifts as a reward,
> surely more splendid
> than you sought to have.

And then he said:

> To good Fridthjof,
> I give my wife,
> and with her,
> my wealth all.

Fridthjof spoke a verse:

> I will not take
> these treasures,
> unless, famed one,
> you were fatally ill.

The king answered, "I would not have given you that unless that was so— I am ill. And I make this arrangement with her for you to enjoy, because you are above most men. Now I will grant you the title of king, because her brothers will not bestow such honors upon you. Now pledge yourself to my wife."

Fridthjof said, "You have my thanks for that, lord, but I will not bear a higher distinction than the title of jarl."

The king died soon after, but Fridthjof held his own wedding, and then the king's funeral-feast was held. Then he settled down to govern the land, and seemed to be a most greatly renowned man, and he and Ingibjorg had children together. Fridthjof was called a jarl.

And when her brothers heard that, Helgi said to his brother, "Such is a great abomination, that an ignoble man should have our sister. Now we will go and get her out of his hands, and prevent these evil spells."

And so they did, they summoned great forces and went against Fridthjof. When he heard that, he said to the queen, "Now we may expect trouble on our hands. However matters go, I don't want you to be displeased."

She answered, "It has come to this: I want to lose you least of all."

Then they went into battle, and Fridthjof went forward so fiercely that he was foremost of his men, and he met Helgi and they fought fiercely, and in the end Helgi fell, and then the victory-call was sounded.

Then Fridthjof said, "You have two choices, Halfdan, to accept a settlement or suffer death. But now it seems that I have better cause than you two brothers."

Halfdan said that he would choose that, and he went home to his kingdom, and he had to yield tribute to Fridthjof forever after. But Fridthjof settled down in his lands and was the most famous man on account of his valor, and he had many children with his wife and lived to be an old man.

> And so this saga must end.
> Good days to us may Our Lord send,
> and may we receive that peace,
> may all blessings never cease.
> May mother Mary guard us long,
> with the angels, good and strong.
> May the Redeemer never fail
> to lead our steps on heaven's trail.
> Our dearest Lord will send
> good life to me without end,
> towards happiness in peace to wend.
> *Amen ad eterne*
> *et mi pater et mater,*
> *bona soror et frater.*[7]

NOTES

Introduction

1 Tegnér, *Frithiof's Saga: A Legend of the North*, pp. 1-39.
2 Morris and Magnússon, *Three Northern Love Stories*, pp. 65-114.
3 Anderson and Bjarnasson, *Viking Tales of the North*, pp. 75-111.
4 Sephton, "A Translation of the Saga of Frithiof the Fearless." *Proceedings of the Liverpool Literary and Philosophical Society* vol. 48, pp.
5 Kalinké, "Norse Romance," pp. 316-317.
6 Craigie, *The Icelandic Sagas*, p. 95.
7 Koht, *The Old Norse Sagas*, pp. 152-153.
8 Schlauch, *Medieval Narrative*, pp. 5-33.
9 http://www.fridtjov.no/
10 Driscoll and Hufnagel, "*Fornaldarsögur norðurlanda.*"
11 Evans, "*Friðþjófs saga ins frækna*", p. 221.
12 Kalinké, "Norse Romance", pp. 345-349.
13 See Quinn, "Interrogating Genre", for a recent overview of opinions.
14 Ross, *Prolonged Echoes*, vol. 2, pp. 50-51; O'Connor, *Icelandic Histories and Romances*, pp. 41-46; Waggoner, *Sagas of Ragnar Lodbrok*, pp. xi-xiv.
15 Mitchell, *Heroic Sagas*, p. 27.
16 Mitchell, *Heroic Sagas*, pp. 27-29.
17 Kalinké, *Bridal-Quest Romance*, pp. 121-123.
18 Kalinké, *Bridal-Quest Romance*, pp. 107-108.
19 Kalinké, *Bridal-Quest Romance*, pp. 115-120.
20 Kalinké, *Bridal-Quest Romance*, p. 115.
21 *Lagom* is a Swedish word meaning something like "just the right thing."

Notes

22 Tegnér, "Introductory Letter to Frithiof's Saga", *Frithiof's Saga: A Legend of the North*, p. 45.
23 *Frithiof's Saga*, canto XV, verse 14, p. 151.
24 *Frithiof's Saga*, canto XXIV, verse 33, p. 224.
25 Goethe, *Ueber Kunst und Alterthum*, p. 143.
26 [Longfellow, Review of *Frithiofs Saga*], pp. 150-152.
27 Longfellow, "Tegnér's Drapa", *Poems*, pp. 649-650.
28 [Longfellow, Review of *Frithiofs Saga*], p. 151.
29 Appelmann, "Relation", pp. 165-180.
30 "Recent Literature", p. 499.
31 Grove, *Dictionary*, vol. 4, p. 677.
32 *Dwight's Journal of Music*, March 1, 1879, p. 39.
33 Boston Symphony Orchestra, *Thirty-Eighth Season Programme*, April 11, 1919, p. 1165.
34 Andrée, *Fritiof Suite / Symphony in A Minor*, Stockholm Symphony Orchestra, cond. Gustav Sjokvist. Sterling CDS 1016-2.
35 Ægir is the Norse sea-god, and also—probably not coincidentally—the name of a German warship, *SMS Ägir*, launched in 1896. Her sister ship *SMS Frithjof* had already been commissioned in 1893.
36 Blind, "The 'Song to Aegir'", p. 95.
37 "A Week's Musical Topics", p. 21.
38 Wawn, *Vikings and Victorians*, pp. 127-128.
39 Longfellow, "Tegnér's Drapa", *Poems*, p. 648.
40 Lewis, *Surprised by Joy*, p. 17.
41 Lewis, p. 73.
42 Lewis, p. 77.
43 Lewis, "Religion Without Dogma?", *God in the Dock*, p. 132.
44 Quoted in Wawn, *Vikings and Victorians*, p. 130.
45 Conybeare, *The Place of Iceland*, p. 4.
46 Wawn, *Vikings and Victorians*, especially ch. 8.
47 Ballantyne, *Erling the Bold*, p. 437.
48 Canto 2, verse 10; p. 18.
49 *Edda*, ch. 22.
50 Turville-Petre, *Myth and Religion of the North*, pp. 119-120.
51 *History of the Danes* III.70-77, trans. Ellis-Davidson and Fisher, pp. 69-75.
52 *Frithiof's Saga*, canto XXIV, verse 28, p. 220.

Sagas of Fridthjof

53   Turville-Petre, pp. 116-118.
54   *Hauks páttr Hábrókar*, trans. Bachman, *Forty Old Icelandic Tales*, pp. 9-14.
55   *Sagan af Þjalar-Jóni*, ed. Gunnlaug Þórðarson.
56   Garmonsway, *Beowulf and its Analogues*, pp. 327-328.
57   Motif D732, in Thompson, *Motif Index of Folk Literature*, vol. 2, p. 84.
58   Motif Z116, in Thompson, vol. 5, p. 560; MacKillop, "Sovereignty, Lady", *Dictionary of Celtic Mythology*, pp. 344-345.
59   Simek, "*Þorsteins saga Víkingssonar*", p. 675.
60   *Egils saga* ch. 64.
61   *Víga-Glúms saga* ch. 4.
62   *Flóamanna saga* chs. 15, 17.
63   O'Donoghue, *Old Norse-Icelandic Literature*, p. 101.
64   Tulinius, quoted in "Interrogating Genre", pp. 279-280.
65   Quoted in Wawn, "*Úlfs saga Uggasonar*".
66   Schlauch, *Romance in Iceland*, p. 37.
67   Wawn, *Vikings and Victorians*, p. 120.
68   Driscoll and Hufnagel, "*Fornaldarsögur norðurlanda*."
69   Driscoll, "Late Prose Fiction", pp. 202-203.
70   Kalinké, "Genesis of Fiction", pp. 10-12; Vermeyden, "Gautreks saga", pp. 224-225.
71   Jónsson and Vilhjálmsson, *Fornaldarsögur Norðurlanda*, vol. 2, pp. 183-246.
72   Rafn, *Fornaldar Sögur Norðurlanda*, vol. 2, pp. 381-459.
73   Jónsson and Vilhjálmsson, *Fornaldarsögur Norðurlanda*, vol. 2, pp. 247-270.
74   Larsson, *Friðþjófs saga ins Frækna*, pp. xxii-xxiii.
75   Jónsson and Vilhjálmsson, *Fornaldarsögur Norðurlanda*, vol. 3, pp. 1-41.
76   Ranisch, *Die Gautrekssaga*.

The Saga of Thorstein Vikingsson

1   *há-Logi* = "high Logi" or "tall Logi".
2   The Old Norse word for "giant" here is *rís*. Some sagas describe

Notes

the *rísir* as not only large, but handsome and relatively good-natured, if not especially intelligent (e.g. *Örvar-Odds saga* ch. 18). *Barðar saga Snæfellsáss* (ch. 1) contrasts the handsome *rísir* with other sorts of giant, the hostile *tröll* and *þursar*.

3 *Élivágar*, "Winter Storm Waves", appear in Norse cosmology as a river or group of rivers that flow out of Niflheim, the world of primal mist and ice; the first animate being, the giant Ymir, coalesces out of frozen droplets of its venomous or fermenting water. (*Prose Edda, Gylfaginning* 4-5, trans. Faulkes, p. 10; *Vafþrúðnismál'* 31, *Poetic Edda*, trans. Hollander, p. 47). Elivagar is mentioned in a few myths that are set after the creation of the universe; essentially, it's located at "the ends of the earth". See Lindow, *Norse Mythology*, pp. 108-109.

4 *Elfr* is an old word for "river", cognate with the German river name *Elbe*. The Gautelfr is the Göta älv in Sweden; the Raumelfr is now called the Glomma River in Norway. Alfheim thus corresponds roughly to the province of Bohuslän in Sweden.

5 The tradition that the folk of Alfheim were beautiful seems to come from the mythological Alfheim, land of the alfar or elves. See "List of Swedish Kings", trans. Waggoner, *Sagas of Ragnar Lodbrok*, p. 6; *Sögubrot*, ibid., pp. 52, 58; Tolkien, *Saga of King Heidrek*, p. 67.

6 *raumr* is both a poetic term for "giant" and an epithet meaning something like "big clumsy oaf".

7 *eisa* and *eimyrja* both mean "embers". The name of Hálogi's wife Glöð is literally the feminine form of *glaðr*, "glad", but it might be an error for *glóð*, "glowing coal", which would fit Hálogi's fiery nature.

8 *Jómsvíkinga saga* (ch. 13; Hollander, transl., p. 64) mentions Veseti who rules Bornholm, father of Bui and Sigurd Cape; this source gives his wife's name as Hildigunn. But *Jómsvíkinga saga* takes place in historical time, whereas this part of *Þorsteins saga* is set in the indefinite past.

9 *Ullarakr* could be either "Field of Wool" or "Field of Ullr", Ullr being a god associated with winter and archery.

10 The hero or villain who crosses an uncrossable mountain to meet a king also appears in "king's sagas" (e.g. *Hauks þáttr Hábrók* in *Flateyjarbók*, trans. Bachman, *Forty Old Icelandic Tales*, pp. 9-14) and "chivalric sagas" (e.g. *Sagan af Þjalar-Jóni* ch. 2, ed. Gunnlaug Þórðarson, p. 6-7.).

11 *Járnhauss* (Iron-Skull) is also the nickname of a berserk in *Víga-Glúms saga* ch. 6, and of another berserk in *Flóamanna saga* ch. 15. Giants

Sagas of Fridthjof

often have names referring to iron: giants named *Járnnefr* ("Iron Nose") and yet another *Járnhauss* appear in *Hálfdanar saga Brönufostra*, and *Járnskjöldr* ("Iron Shield") is a giant in *Þorsteins þáttr uxafóts*, while the giantess *Járnsaxa* ("Iron Knife") is a concubine of the god Thor.

12 Old Norse *Kolr kroppinbak*. A character named *Kolr krappi* (Kol Hunch) appears as a villain in *Sturlaugs saga starfsama* (chs. 6-10). Like Harek, he demands a desirable woman by threatening her father, he is invulnerable to ordinary weapons, and he is killed by a hero who has been given a special sword.

13 The word *dís* normally means a female guardian spirit or deity.

14 The Norse word translated "sorcery" is *seiðr*. *Seiðr* is a type of magic, sometimes used to foretell the future or to protect someone in battle, but often used to create illusions and confuse enemies. According to Snorri Sturluson (*Ynglinga saga* ch. 7; *Heimskringla*, trans. Hollander, p. 11), its use was considered unmanly (although the god Odin was a master of *seiðr*), and in the legendary sagas it is rarely used for good purposes.

15 *Blámenn*, "black men", appear in several romantic sagas. The word is used in a few historical sagas for black Africans, but the "black men" and "black berserks" of the legendary sagas have virtually nothing to do with actual Africans; they are stock fantasy villains whose primary function is to look exotic and menacing and then be killed by the hero after an exciting battle scene.

16 *Marseraland* appears only in this saga and has not been identified.

17 Possibly the present-day Grønsund, northeast of the island of Falster in Denmark.

18 The theme of a man who is betrothed to a desirable woman, makes her wait for three years while he travels, and loses her to a rival is found in several "skalds' sagas", such as *Gunnlaugs saga ormstungu* and *Bjarnar saga Hítdælakappa*. In those sagas, this theme is the main plot and it usually ends tragically; here, it is just one of many episodes, and it ends happily.

19 *Solbjört* means "sun-bright".

20 Old Norse *Svafa*; meaning conjectural.

21 The *herör* or "war-arrow" was an arrow that was passed from home to home as a summons to join a military levy. The custom is mentioned in many historical sagas as well as legendary ones.

Notes

22 *Bálagarðssíð* is mentioned in both historical and legendary sagas (e.g. *Harðar saga* ch. 17; *Óláfs saga helga* ch. 7), but is usually associated with magic and monsters. It was apparently somewhere in the eastern Baltic.

23 This method of putting sorcerous women to death appears in a few other sagas, notably *Eyrbyggja saga* ch. 20; the bag is presumably to prevent the woman from putting the evil eye on her killers.

24 Killing under cover of darkness was regarded as murder under Norse custom and law; *Egils saga* (ch. 59) states that *náttvíg eru morðvíg*, "night-killings are murders".

25 The shallow passage between the northernmost part of Jutland and the rest of the mainland.

26 In *Örvar-Odds saga* ch. 9 the scene is repeated: Hjalmar ceases fighting with Odd when he finds that Odd's raiding has gained him little wealth, saying *vér berjumst um ekki nema kapp ok metnað* ("we're fighting over nothing but reputation and pride").

27 The modern island of Tromøy, Norway.

28 Mæfil the sea-king is briefly mentioned in *Hversu Nóregr Byggðist*, ch. 1.

29 A *hersir* is a local leader, in the service of a jarl or king.

30 *Vágar* means "the bays"; it's a common place-name in the Norse world.

31 Presumably the same as the Ingjald Bad-Ruler whose bloody career is told in *Ynglinga saga* 34-40 (transl. Hollander, *Heimskringla*, pp. 36-43).

32 *Knáttleikr* was played with a ball and bats. Mentioned in several sagas of Icelanders as well as legendary sagas, it was evidently a popular sport. The saga descriptions are not detailed enough to reconstruct the rules, but it may have been similar to the Irish game of hurling.

33 Norse idiom meaning "no one will kill you"—i.e. no one will cut off your head and step on it.

34 The god Odin was said to wear a dark blue (*blár*) cloak. Characters in sagas wear dark blue clothing when in a killing mood (*Víga-Glúms saga* ch. 6; *Njáls saga* ch. 92; *Hrafnkels saga* chs. 6, 18), and according to *Þiðreks saga*, wearing *blár* is the sign of "a cold breast and a grim heart" (ch. 174; ed. Bertelsen, p. 328).

35 The names Gautan and Ogautan mean "Bragging" and "Not

Bragging".

36 Persons who can send out their *fylgjar* to fight or to gather information (see Note 38 below) must usually be asleep or in trance; waking them has serious consequences. (e.g. *Hrólfs saga kraka*, ch. 33, trans. Byock. pp. 74-75; *Hjálmpés saga ok Ölvis* ch. 11, trans. O'Connor, *Icelandic Histories & Romances*, p. 164-166)

37 Possibly a direct or indirect borrowing of Aeolus's bag of winds in the *Odyssey* (10:19-24; trans. Murray, vol. 1, pp. 358-361). This wouldn't be the only Homeric borrowing in the sagas: episodes in *Hrólfs saga Gautrekssonar* (ch. 19) and *Egils saga einhenda* (ch. 10) are borrowed from the episode in the cave of Polyphemus.

38 The fetch (Old Norse *fylgja*, literally "follower") is a spirit that attends each person, usually taking the shape of an animal whose nature resembles that of the person. In the sagas, fetches are seen in dreams, as portents, but are rarely seen in waking life, although persons who are shape-shifters may be able to send their fetches out into the world (which is apparently what Ogautan does in Chapter XIII). Powerful warriors often have bears as fetches; exceptionally mighty men may have bears with red cheeks (cf. *Hrólfs saga Gautrekssonar* ch. 7).

39 The fictional *Íslendingasaga*, *Víglundar saga* (chs. 16-17), contains a similar episode; the brothers Víglund and Trausti win a battle against lopsided odds, collapse from exhaustion, but in the end are rescued by their father, who comes for them with a sledge over the ice and hides them in an underground room.

40 *bikkjustakkr*, "bitch-skin", is defined in Cleasby and Vigfusson's *Dictionary* as simply an insult. But shape-shifting by magically endowed persons was thought to involve altering one's skin or putting a new skin on (e.g. the expressions *hamrammr*, "skin-strong", and *eigi einhamr*, "not of one skin", for a shape-shifter), and *bikkjustakkr* probably refers to Ogautan's vixen shape.

41 *Sámr* = "swarthy"; *Fullafli* = "fully capable" or "fully powerful".

42 A similar incident appears in *Hrólfs saga Gautrekssonar* ch. 19: Hrolf's men take shelter in the hut of a giant, who later comes home with the carcass of a bear, and who offers the men food and lodging but promises to torture hem in the morning. More distant analogues appear in *Ketils saga hængs* ch. 2 and *Göngu-Hrólfs saga* ch. 5.

43 In *Grettis saga* chs. 32-35, the undead Glámr terrorizes people by

riding on the roofs of houses until they nearly break. Such a belief about the undead may be at the root of the people's fear here.

44 Judicial duels (*hólmganga*) were fought with both combatants standing on a spread-out cloak, or otherwise in a ritually defined and confined space. A combatant who stepped off the cloak lost the duel. See *Kormaks saga* ch. 10 for a detailed description.

45 *Haraldr kesja*, Harald Pike or Harald Halberd, was also the name of a son of King Erik Evergood of Denmark, born in 1080 and killed in 1135. Harald married the daughter of Magnus Barefoot. (*Haraldssona saga* ch. 5, in *Heimskringla*, trans. Hollander, p. 740) His connection, if any, with the legendary figure briefly mentioned in this saga is unknown.

46 *Skellinefja* means something like "rattling nose". Several giants in the legendary sagas have names referring to their outlandish noses, such as *Arinnefja* ("eagle nose" or "eagle-beak"), *Skinnnefja* ("skin-nose"), *Hornnefja* ("horn nose"), and *Járnnefr* ("iron nose").

47 In the more romantic sagas, it's common for a person who is being cursed to have the opportunity to cast a counter-curse. See Schlauch, *Romance in Iceland*, pp. 132-133.

48 The Norse text reads *Valland*, the usual word for northern France, corresponding more or less to Normandy and Brittany.

49 Although runes aren't mentioned by name, *kefli* is the usual word for a rune-carved stick. In the sagas, runes carved on a stick or other object may simply convey a message, but are sometimes used for magical purposes, including making a woman fall in love with someone; see *Egils saga* chs. 73, 77.

50 Giantesses in the legendary sagas are often depicted wearing ragged, immodest attire that reveals or nearly reveals the buttocks; for example, *Illuga saga Griðarfóstra* ch. 4; *Gríms saga loðinkinna* ch. 2.

51 *Illuga saga Griðarfóstra* ch. 6 also features a giantess who befriends the hero, who hangs a villain from his ship's mast, and who turns out to be a princess in disguise.

52 This episode with Skellinefja closely resembles an episode in *Gríms saga loðinkinna* ch. 2, in which Grim is rescued and healed by a hideous giantess who is really his betrothed under an enchantment.

53 *Slysa-Úfi* means something like "Bad Luck Ufi".

54 *Ötunfaxi* probably means "Unclean Mane".

Sagas of Fridthjof

55 A proverb. See also *Kjalnesinga saga* ch. 9.

56 Literally *jarðarmen*, "necklace of the earth"; this is a long strip of turf cut so that it can be raised into an arch, with its ends still attached to the ground. Passing beneath it, and mingling blood, were part of the rite of blood-brotherhood; similar rituals are described in the sagas of Icelanders (e.g. *Gísla saga Súrssonar* ch. 6; *Fóstbræðra saga* ch. 2).

57 A fairly common literary device for whitewashing a hero's raiding career—for example, *Friðþjófs saga inn frækna* ch. 11; *Sturlaugs saga starfsama* ch. 4.

58 Probably the present-day island of Brännö, in the Göteborg Islands at the mouth of the Göta älv.

59 Literally, "You might comb no proper tent-pegs for them."

60 *Dísir* are female spirits associated with a person; they may protect him or cause his downfall. *Dísir* seem to be inherited along family lines. In some sources, the concept of the *dísir* seems to overlap with the fetch or *fylgja* (see Note 38 above), which usually appears as an animal but sometimes is said to appear in female form. See Lindow, *Norse Mythology*, pp. 95-97, for an overview of the sources.)

61 A few other sagas feature a powerful magical being who is said to shoot arrows from every finger; for example, the two goddesses Thorgerd and Irpa do this in *Jómsvíkinga saga* ch. 21 (trans. Hollander, p. 101).

62 Old Norse *Papey*, "island of the Irish hermits"—*pápar* being the Norse name for the Irish religious hermits who colonized remote islands throughout the north Atlantic, including Iceland.

63 See Note 24 about how killing someone by night was considered unlawful.

64 This episode was probably borrowed from *Örvar-Odds saga* ch. 16, in which Örvar-Odd asks a similar question about who will entertain whom.

65 *hasla völl*, literally "to hazel a field", was done before a duel: the boundaries of the dueling ground were marked out with hazel stakes (e.g. *Kormaks saga* ch. 10). Evidently this was also done before some larger battles (e.g. *Egils saga* ch. 52; *Hákonar saga góða* ch. 24 and *Óláfs saga Tryggvasonar* ch. 18, in *Heimskringla*). It may be that hazeling the field meant that the battle was meant to settle a dispute once and for all, as a judicial duel was supposed to do.

66 *vé-freyja* means "lady (or goddess) of the temple." Someone of that name appears in *Sturlaugs saga starfsama* and its sequel *Göngu-Hrólfs saga*; it's not clear whether she is intended to be the same person, but in *Sturlaugs saga* she does own a magic sword, although its original name is not given.

The Saga of Fridthjof the Bold

1 *Fóstbræðr* can mean either "foster brothers" (men raised by the same foster-father) or "sworn brothers" (men who have sworn an oath of brotherhood, regardless of where they were raised). It's not always clear which sense is meant, but since the text doesn't state that Hilding raised Bjorn and Asmund together with Fridthjof, as he did with Ingibjorg, I have assumed that Bjorn and Asmund are Fridthjof's sworn brothers.
2 To "sit on a burial mound" (*sitja á haugi*) is usually depicted as a rite by which one may gain wisdom from the dead. But in some later sagas (e.g. *Gautreks saga* ch. 8, trans. Pálsson and Edwards, *Seven Viking Romances*, p. 160; *Göngu-Hrolfs saga* ch. 5, trans. Pálsson and Edwards, pp. 38-39; *Hjálmpes saga ok Ölvis* ch. 1, trans. O'Connor, *Icelandic Histories & Romances*, p. 117) it has no obvious magical significance. Here it may only be a sign that the kings are trying to assert their father's authority.
3 In the shorter version of this saga, Hring is the king of Sweden.
4 In the shorter saga, the kings send unnamed messengers to ask for Fridthjof's help.
5 *Hnefatafl* is a game played on a square board, superficially resembling chess but very different in detail. See Bell, *Board and Table Games*, pp. 78-81, for a brief overview, or Bayless, "Alea, Tæfl, and Related Games", for a much more comprehensive study.
6 The verb Fridthjof uses here is *bregða*, which connotes a quick or tricky maneuver. A related idiom, *brögð í tafli*, "moves on the game board", means "there's trickery afoot".
7 The text literally reads *rauðr*, "red", but the Norse word covered shades of brown, orange, and yellow, as well as what English speakers now call red. *Rauðr* was commonly used to describe gold, and gold

was often compared to beautiful women.
8 In southeast Norway, near the present-day city of Stavanger.
9 Note that in the shorter saga, the exchange of rings takes place before Fridthjof asks Ingibjorg's brothers for her hand in marriage.
10 The expression "to enjoy one's self" (*skemmta sér*) sometimes, but not always, has sexual connotations. (Jochens, *Women in Old Norse Society*, pp. 68-69)
11 The Norse word is *dísarsal*, "hall of the *dís* (singular)". *Dísir* are female spirits who were the object of worship; some sagas mention a *dísablót* (a sacrifice to the *dísir*) held in a *dísasalr*, a hall of the *dísir* (e.g. *Ynglinga saga* ch. 29, trans. Hollander, *Heimskringla*, p. 33). Some texts portray the *dísir* as spirits associated with a family or lineage, sometimes protecting their people and sometimes sealing their doom. But *dís* may also mean "goddess", appearing in poetic names for goddesses (such as *Vanadís* for Freyja). See Lindow, *Norse Mythology*, pp. 93-97.
12 Norse *seiðkonur*, "*seiðr*-women." *Seiðr* is a form of magic, sometimes used to foretell future events or protect persons, but often used to create illusions or affect victims' minds. *Seiðr* generally has a sinister reputation in the sagas. Several sagas describe *seiðr* as being done from atop a platform (*seiðhjallr*) or other high place.
13 *Heiðr* is a common name for witches; *Hamgláma* means "skin-illusion", "skin-glamour", implying that this sorceress is a shapeshifter (Old Norse *hamhleypa*). Note that the witches are not named in the shorter saga.
14 Ægir is described in the *Prose Edda* (*Skáldskaparmál* 25, 33, trans. Faulkes, pp. 91-93, 95) as the god of the sea; his name is also a poetic synonym for the sea itself. See Lindow, *Norse Mythology*, p. 47.
15 The original Norse verse uses end-rhyme, which is unusual in verses like this. My translation follows the rhyme scheme.
16 Rán, "robber", is the name of the wife of the sea god Ægir; the waves were said to be their daughters. The *Prose Edda* claims that she has a net that she uses to capture sailors and drag them down (*Skáldskaparmál* 33, trans. Faulkes, p. 95), and Egil Skallagrimsson's poem *Sonatorrek* blames Rán for the loss of his son by drowning (stanza 7; *Egils saga Skallagrímssonar* ch. 79). See Lindow, *Norse Mythology*, p. 258.
17 Old Norse *Effjusund*.
18 Evie (Old Norse *Effja*) is a town on Orkney mainland. Close by,

Notes

overlooking Eynhallow Sound, is the Broch of Gurness, a large stone tower with outbuildings. The Broch was built well before the Norse came to Orkney, probably in the first century CE. Yet there are other instances of Norsemen knowing and making use of prehistoric stone structures (e.g. *Egils saga* chs. 32-33). It's possible that the saga author knew of a tradition that Gurness had once been the seat of rulers.

19 A proverbial expression.
20 The Norse reads *eyjarskeggjar*, "island-beards". The word is a pejorative, seemingly implying that the islanders are not just bearded but uncouth and bizarre.
21 The expression for "to marry" is literally *drekka bruðlaup*, "to drink the wedding", a common Norse idiom implying that much alcohol was served. See Jochens, *Women in Old Norse Society*, p. 106.
22 The word translated "goddesses" is *dísir*; see Note 11 above.
23 A rather common literary way to whitewash a bloody career; see, e.g. *Þorsteins saga Víkingssonar* ch. 22; *Sturlaugs saga starfsama* ch. 4.
24 "Salt-burning" refers to making salt by burning seaweed, resulting in a black, ashy product. It was considered a very lowly occupation.
25 Fridthjof's disguise may be based on an episode told in Saxo's *History of the Danes* (VI.176-177; trans. Ellis-Davidson and Fisher, pp. 165-166), in which the commoner and poet Hjarni disguises himself as a salt-burner and infiltrates the court of the Danish king Fridleif—although his motivation is different from Fridthjof's, and his fate is more tragic.
26 Fridthjof calls himself *Þjófr*, meaning "thief", and says that he was with *Úlfr*, which means "wolf" and has connotations of outlawry and savagery, but is also a fairly common man's name. Fridthjof's name for his homeland is *Angr*, which is a pun: it means "narrow fjord" (as in modern Norwegian place names such as Stavanger and Hardanger) but also "sorrow; grief."
27 *Friðr* means "peace and security", but it may be a pun on *firðir*, "fjords", in response to Fridthjof's pun on *Angr*. It's also a pun on Fridthjof's real name—Fridthjof is using the last part of his name, *Þjófr* or "thief", as an alias, but the king's use of the first part of his name suggests that he knows very well who his guest really is.
28 This sentence alliterates in the Norse, and I've retained the alliteration here.

29 This episode may have been inspired by the Biblical story of David, who has an opportunity to kill Saul but spares him (1 Samuel 24:1-22). However, it seems closer to an incident in the *Alexiad*, a history written by the Byzantine scholar Anna Comnena. (Schauch, *Romance in Iceland*, pp. 63-64; Kalinké, *Bridal-Quest Romance*, pp. 117-121)

30 A minor chieftain, ranking lower than a jarl.

31 A frequent source of tragedy in Norse and Anglo-Saxon literature is the woman caught up in hostility between her husband and her kinfolk, torn in her loyalties and unable to keep the peace. Examples include Hildeburh in *Beowulf* and Gudrun in the Völsung legend. Ingibjorg is making her loyalties very clear here.

32 Several sagas mention "peace-shields" (*friðskildi*) or "war-shields" (*herskildi*). *Eiríks saga rauða* (chs. 10-11) mentions that red shields were used by a hostile force, while white shields were a token of peace.

The Tale of King Vikar

1 These events are also told in one version of *Heiðreks saga*, which adds that Alfhild was carrying out a sacrifice to the *dísir* (female spirits) when abducted, and claims that Alfhild's child by Starkad Ala-Warrior was a girl named Bauggerd. (Tolkien, *Saga of King Heidrek*, pp. 66-67)

2 Now Tromøy, off the coast of Arendal in southern Norway.

3 "Coal-biter" (*kolbítr*) is the usual epithet for an unpromising young man who does nothing but sit idly by the fire. In many sagas, a coal-biter ends up becoming a great hero when forced to rise to the occasion. The *kolbítr* bears a certain resemblance to the *askeladden* ("ash-lad") or *askefisen* ("ash-fart") of Norwegian folktales.

4 The *svínfylking*, literally "swine-formation", is the usual Norse name for the wedge formation, because of its supposed resemblance to a pig's head. Odin teaches it to kings whom he favors (Saxo, *History of the Danes* I.32, p. 31, VII.248-249, pp. 226-227; *Sögubrot* ch 8, trans. Waggoner, *Sagas of Ragnar Lodbrok*, p. 54; *Reginsmál* 23, trans. Hollander, *Poetic Edda*, p. 222.) Although this is not explicitly stated, the fact that Vikar is using the wedge is probably meant to suggest his close relationship with Odin.

5 "To cast wood-chips" (*falla spán*) refers to a rite of divination. In other

Notes

texts the expression is *falla blótspán*, "to cast sacrificial wood-chips," suggesting that the rite was associated with religious sacrifices.

6 Snorri Sturluson's *Prose Edda* also mentions an assembly of twelve gods. This resembles the Twelve Olympians of classical Greek mythology and the Dii Consentes of Roman mythology, and Snorri, and the author of this tale, may have been borrowed the concept directly or indirectly from classical sources.

7 *Skáldatal*, a list of ancient poets preserved in some manuscripts of the *Prose Edda*, lists Starkad at the beginning, and calls his poems "the most ancient of those which people now know" (quoted in Clunies-Ross, "Poet into Myth", p. 31).

8 In *Styrbjarnar þáttr Svíakappa*, a tale in the *Flateyjarbók*, Odin gives King Eirek a reed, which turns into a spear when he throws it and speaks the words "Odin has you all!" (*Fornmanna Sögur* vol. 5, p. 250) The myth of the death of Odin's son Balder, of course, also features a weak plant turning into a deadly weapon (*Edda, Gylfaginning* 49; trans. Faulkes, pp. 48-49).

9 Saxo Grammaticus tells much the same story of Vikar's death, but with some differences: In Saxo's account, only Odin is involved in setting Starkad's destiny and makes him commit dastardly deeds; Vikar is hanged with willow branches (Saxo mentions a tradition that has them turning into iron bands at the crucial moment); and Starkad stabs Vikar with his sword instead of the reed-spear. (*History of the Danes* VI.184; trans. Ellis-Davidson and Fisher, pp. 170-171)

10 A *thul* (Old Norse *þulr*) is an official of the king, whose role included giving advice, remembering and reciting old lore, and mediating between gods and men. Russel Poole has pointed out that Starkad's poem *Víkarsbálkr*, along with other poems and acts of Starkad preserved in Saxo's *History of the Danes*, contain very much the sort of knowledge and counsel that a thul would be expected to provide (cited in Clunies-Ross, "Poet into Myth", pp. 34-36). It's ironic that Starkad calls himself a "silent thul", since the word is related to Old Norse *þylja*, "utter", and its Old English cognate *þyle* is glossed as Latin *orator*; speaking advice, poetry, lore, and speeches to rouse or calm the other men was apparently a key part of the thul's role (Enright, "The Warband Context of the Unferth Episode").

11 One version of *Heiðreks saga* states that Starkad Ala-Warrior, the

grandfather of the Starkad who speaks this poem, had eight arms, and also tells of how he killed Hergrim in single combat (Tolkien, *Saga of King Heidrek*, pp. 66-67). Saxo Grammaticus knew of a tradition in which Thor tore all but two arms from a multi-armed giant named Starkad, which is evidently what the poem refers to—although Saxo identified the multi-armed giant with Starkad the speaker of this poem, not his grandfather. (*History of the Danes* VI.183, trans. Ellis-Davidson and Fisher, p. 170)

12 This episode is also told in *Ynglinga saga* ch. 20 (*Heimskringla*, transl. Hollander, p. 23).

The Shorter Fridthjof's Saga

1 The word *tafl* means any board game (it comes from Latin *tabula*, which originally meant a game similar to backgammon). In the longer version of this saga, the game is identified as the specific game *hnefatafl*; see Note 7 for the longer saga.

2 There is an untranslatable pun in this line: the waves are described as *úrigi*, meaning both "wet" and "bad-tempered."

3 A breach of etiquette while drinking in a hall might be penalized by forcing the person to drain an extra horn, the *vítishorn* or "penalty horn." (Jochens, *Women in Old Norse Society*, p. 109)

4 The type of magic that the witches are working here was known as *seiðr*. It was commonly depicted as being worked from a high seat or platform (*seiðhjallr*). See Note 12 to the longer saga of Fridthjof.

5 *Svölnir* is a name of Odin; his *maids* are presumably valkyries. Presumably the temple is meant by this kenning; although it is supposedly a temple to Balder, Odin's son, the longer version of the saga clarifies the matter by setting this scene in the *dísarsal*, the "hall of the goddess".

6 The text as published reads *grunskjöldungar*, which could be "suspicious kings" (literally, "suspicious Skjoldungs", the Skjoldungs being a famed dynasty whose name can be used poetically for any kings). But other editors (e.g. Falk, "Om Friðþjófs saga," p. 82) suggest *grundskjöldungar*, "ground-kings" or "land-kings", and I've followed this emendation here.

7 "Amen in eternity, and my father and mother, good sister and brother." The Latin is not quite grammatically correct.

BIBLIOGRAPHY

Note that Icelandic authors have been alphabetized by first name, as is common practice. Also note that all Icelandic sagas mentioned in the text or footnotes, whose publication information is not specifically cited, may be found in *Complete Sagas of Icelanders*, edited by Viðar Hreinsson.

Anderson, Rasmus B., and Jón Bjarnason. *Viking Tales of the North: The Sagas of Thorstein, Viking's Son, and Fridthjof the Bold*. Chicago: S. C. Griggs and Co., 1877.

Appelmann, Anton. "The Relation of Longfellow's *Evangeline* to Tegnér's *Frithiofs saga*." *Scandinavian Studies*, vol. 2, no. 3 (1915), pp. 165-180.

"A Week's Musical Topics: Timely Gossip of the Concert Halls and Opera Houses." *The New York Times*, November 28, 1894, p. 21.

Bachman, W. Bryant, Jr. *Forty Old Icelandic Tales*. Lanham, Md.: University Press of America, 1992.

Ballantyne, Robert M. *Erling the Bold: A Tale of the Norse Sea-Kings*. Philadelphia: J. B. Lippincott, 1883.

Bayless, Martha. "Alea, Tæfl, and Related Games: Vocabulary and Context," in *Latin Learning and English Lore*, ed. Katherine O'Brien O'Keeffe and Andy Orchard, 2 vols. (University of Toronto Press, 2005), II, pp. 9-27.

Bibliography

Bell, R. C. *Board and Table Games from Many Civilizations.* London: Oxford University Press, 1960.

Blind, Karl. "The 'Song to Aegir'". *The Scottish Review,* vol. 27 (1896), pp. 95-104.

Boston Symphony Orchestra, *Thirty-Eighth Season Programme,* 1918-1919.

Byock, Jesse L., trans. *The Saga of King Hrolf Kraki.* London: Penguin, 1998.

Cleasby, Richard and Gudbrand Vígfusson. *An Icelandic-English Dictionary.* Oxford: Clarendon Press, 1874.

Clunies-Ross, Margaret. "Poet into Myth: Starkaðr and Bragi." *Viking and Medieval Scandinavia,* vol. 2 (2006), pp. 31-43.

Conybeare, C. A. Vansittart. *The Place of Iceland in the History of European Institutions: Being the Lothian Prize Essay, 1877.* Oxford and London: James Parker & Co., 1877.

Craigie, William A. *The Icelandic Sagas.* Cambridge: Cambridge University Press; New York: G. P. Putnam's Sons, 1913.

Driscoll, M. J. and Silvia Hufnagel. "*Fornaldarsögur Norðurlanda*: a Bibliography of Manuscripts, Editions, Translations and Secondary Literature." Arnamagnæan Institute, Copenhagen. http://www.staff.hum.ku.dk/mjd/fornaldarsagas/

Enright, Michael J. "The Warband Context of the Unferth Episode." *Speculum,* vol. 73 (1998), pp. 297-337.

Evans, Jonathan D. M. "*Friðþjófs saga ins frækna.*" *Medieval Scandinavia.* Ed. Phillip Pulsiano and Kirsten Wolf. London: Routledge, 1993. p. 221.

Falk, Hjalmar. "Om Friðþjófs saga." *Arkiv för nordisk filologi: Ny föjld*, vol. 2 (1890), pp. 60-102.

Garmonsway, George Norman, Jacqueline Simpson, and Hilda Roderick Ellis Davidson. *Beowulf and its Analogues*. New York: E. P. Dutton & Co., 1971.

Goethe, Johann Wolfgang. *Ueber Kunst und Alterthum*, vol. 5. Stuttgart: Cotta, 1824.

Grove, Sir George. *A Dictionary of Music and Musicians*. 4 vols. London and New York: Macmillan and Co., 1889.

Guðni Jónsson and Bjarni Vilhjálmson, eds. *Fornaldarsögur Norðurlanda*. 3 vols. Reykjavík: Bókaútgáfan Forni, 1943.

Gunnlaug Þórðarson, ed. *Sagan af Þjalar-Jóni*. Reykjavík: E. Þórðarson, 1857.

Hollander, Lee M., ed. trans. —, ed. *Jómsvíkinga saga*. Austin: University of Texas Press, 1955.

—. *The Poetic Edda*. 2nd ed. Austin: University of Texas Press, 1962.

Homer. *The Odyssey*. 2 vols. Ed. trans. A. T. Murray, rev. George E. Dimock. Loeb Classical Library. Cambridge, Mass.: Harvard University Press, 1995.

Jochens, Jenny. *Women in Old Norse Society*. Ithaca, N.Y. and London: Cornell University Press, 1995.

Kalinké, Marianne E. *Bridal-Quest Romance in Medieval Iceland*. Ithaca, N.Y. and London: Cornell University Press, 1990.

—. "Norse Romance (*riddarasögur*)." *Old Norse–Icelandic Literature: A Critical Guide*. Ed. Carol J. Clover and John Lindow. Toronto:

University of Toronto Press / Medieval Academy of America, 2005. pp. 316-363.

— . "The Genesis of Fiction in the North." *Proceedings of the 13th International Saga Conference, Durham and York, 6th-12th August, 2006*. http://www.dur.ac.uk/medieval.wwww/sagaconf/kalinke.htm

Koht, Halvdan. *The Old Norse Sagas*. New York: W. W. Norton, 1931.

Larson, Ludvig, ed. *Altnordische Saga-Bibliothek. Heft 9: Friðþjófs saga ins Frækna*. Gustaf Cederschiöld, Hugo Gering, and Eugen Mogk, eds. Halle: Max Niemeyer, 1901.

Lewis, C. S. *Surprised by Joy: The Shape of my Early Life*. New York: Harcourt, Brace & World, 1955.

Lewis, C. S. *God in the Dock: Essays on Theology and Ethics*. Grand Rapids, Mich.: Eerdsmans, 1970.

Lindow, John. *Norse Mythology: A Guide to the Gods, Heroes, Rituals, and Beliefs*. Oxford: Oxford University Press, 2002.

Longfellow, Henry Wadsworth. [Review of *Frithiofs Saga*.] *The North American Review*, vol. 45 (1837), pp. 149-185.

Longfellow, Henry Wadsworth. *The Poems of Henry Wadsworth Longfellow*. Modern Library. New York: Random House, 1960.

Mitchell, Stephen A. *Heroic Sagas and Ballads*. Ithaca, N.Y. and London: Cornell University Press, 1991.

Morris, William, and Eiríkur Magnússon. *Three Northern Love Stories and Other Tales*. London: Ellis and White, 1875.

Norræna Fornfræða Félagi. *Fornmanna sögur. Fimta Bindi: Saga Ólafs konúngs hins helga. Önnur deild*. Copenhagen: Popp, 1830.

O'Connor, Ralph, ed. trans. *Icelandic Histories & Romances*. 2nd ed. Stroud, Gloucestershire: Tempus, 2006.

O'Donoghue, Heather. *Old Norse-Icelandic Literature: A Short Introduction*. Oxford: Blackwell, 2004.

Pálsson, Hermann, and Paul Edwards. *Göngu-Hrolfs Saga: A Viking Romance*. Edinburgh: Canongate, 1980.

—. *Seven Viking Romances*. London: Penguin, 1985.

Quinn, Judy, ed. "Interrogating Genre in the *Fornaldarsögur*: Round-Table Discussion." *Viking and Medieval Studies*, vol. 2 (2006), pp. 275-96.

Ranisch, Wilhelm. *Die Gautrekssaga in zwei Fassungen*. Palaestra vol. 11. Berlin: Mayer & Müller, 1900.

"Recent Literature." *The Atlantic Monthly*. Vol. 39, no. 234 (April 1877), pp. 498-510.

Ross, Margaret Clunies. *Prolonged Echoes: Old Norse Myths in Medieval Northern Society. Volume 2: The Reception of Norse Myths in Medieval Iceland*. Odense: Odense University Press, 1998.

—. "Poet into myth: Starkad and Bragi." *Viking and Medieval Scandinavia* vol. 2, no. 2, pp. 31-43.

Saxo Grammaticus. *The History of the Danes: Books I-IX*. Ed. Hilda R. Ellis-Davidson, trans. Peter Fisher. Rochester, N.Y.: D.S. Brewer, 1996.

Schlauch, Margaret. *Medieval Narrative: A Book of Translations*. New York: Prentice-Hall, 1928.

—. *Romance in Iceland*. Princeton, N.J.: Princeton University Press, 1934.

Sephton, John. "A Translation of the Saga of Frithiof the Fearless." *Proceedings of the Liverpool Literary and Philosophical Society*, 1893-4. Vol. 48, pp. 69-98.

Simek, Rudolf. "*Þorsteins saga Víkingssonar.*" *Medieval Scandinavia.* Ed. Phillip Pulsiano and Kirsten Wolf. London: Routledge, 1993. p. 675.

Snorri Sturluson. *Heimskringla: History of the Kings of Norway.* Trans. Lee M. Hollander. Austin: University of Texas Press, 1992.

Tegnér, Esaias. *Frithiof's Saga: A Legend of the North.* Translated by George Stephens. Stockholm: A. Bonnier; London: Black and Armstrong, 1839.

Thompson, Stith. *Motif-Index of Folk-Literature.* 5 vols. Bloomington: Indiana University Press, 1973.

Tolkien, Christopher, ed. trans. *The Saga of King Heidrek the Wise.* London: Thomas Nelson and Sons, 1960.

Turville-Petre, E. O. G. *Myth and Religion of the North: The Religion of Ancient Scandinavia.* New York: Holt, Rinehart and Winston, 1964.

Vermeyden, Paula. "*Gautreks saga.*" *Medieval Scandinavia.* Ed. Phillip Pulsiano and Kirsten Wolf. London: Routledge, 1993. pp. 224-225.

Wawn, Andrew. *The Vikings and the Victorians: Inventing the Old North in 19th-Century Britain.* Cambridge: D. S. Brewer, 2000.

Wawn, Andrew. "Whatever happened to *Úlfs saga Uggasonar?*" *Proceedings of the 13th International Saga Conference, Durham and York, 6th-12th August, 2006.* http://www.dur.ac.uk/medieval.www/sagaconf/wawn.htm

Printed in Great Britain
by Amazon.co.uk, Ltd.,
Marston Gate.